Manmohini Zutshi Sahgal
An Indian Freedom Fighter Recalls Her Life

Autobiographies and Memoirs of Women from Asia, Africa, the Middle East, and Latin America
Geraldine Forbes, Series Editor

SHUDHA MAZUMDAR
MEMOIRS OF AN INDIAN WOMAN
Edited with an Introduction by Geraldine Forbes

CHEN XUEZHAO
SURVIVING THE STORM
A Memoir
Edited with an Introduction by Jeffrey C. Kinkley
Translated by Ti Hua and Caroline Greene

KANEKO FUMIKO
THE PRISON MEMOIRS OF A JAPANESE WOMAN
Translated by Jean Inglis
Introduction by Mikiso Hane

MANMOHINI ZUTSHI SAHGAL
AN INDIAN FREEDOM FIGHTER RECALLS HER LIFE
Edited by Geraldine Forbes
Foreword by B.K. Nehru

THE WOMAN WITH THE ARTISTIC BRUSH
A Life History of Yoruba Batik Artist Nike Olaniyi Davies
Kim Marie Vaz

Manmohini Zutshi Sahgal
An Indian Freedom Fighter Recalls Her Life

Edited by Geraldine Forbes

With a Foreword by B. K. Nehru

An East Gate Book

M.E. Sharpe
Armonk, New York
London, England

An East Gate Book

Copyright © 1994 by Manmohini Zutshi Sahgal

All rights reserved. No part of this book may be reproduced in any form without written permission from the publisher, M. E. Sharpe, Inc., 80 Business Park Drive, Armonk, New York 10504.

Library of Congress Cataloging-in-Publication Data

Sahgal, Manmohini Zutshi, 1909–
An Indian freedom fighter recalls her life / Manmohini Zutshi Sahgal : edited by Geraldine Forbes.
    p.   cm. — (Foremother legacies)
Includes bibliographical references and index.
ISBN 1-56324-339-3. — ISBN 1-56324-340-7 (pbk.)
1. Sahgal, Manmohini Zutshi, 1909–
2. Women social reformers—India—Biography.
3. Women political activists—India—Biography.
4. Kashmiri Pandits—Social life and customs.
5. Women—India—Social conditions.
6. Women—India—Politics and government.
I. Forbes, Geraldine Hancock, 1943–   . II. Title. III. Series.
    HQ1742.S235   1994
    305.42′092—dc20   94-27345
                CIP

Printed in the United States of America

The paper used in this publication meets the minimum requirements of American National Standard for Information Sciences—Permanence of Paper for Printed Library Materials, ANSI Z 39.48-1984.

∞

BM (c) 10 9 8 7 6 5 4 3 2 1
BM (p) 10 9 8 7 6 5 4 3 2 1

This book is dedicated to my late husband, Amrit Sahgal, for his active interest, encouragement, and support throughout our life together, and to my eldest sister, the late Chandra Kumari Handoo, who was especially keen that these memoirs be completed.

Manmohini Sahgal
New Delhi, 1993

Contents

Foreword
  B.K. Nehru — ix
Acknowledgments
  Manmohini Sahgal, Geraldine Forbes — xi
Introduction
  Geraldine Forbes — xiii
The Nehru Family Tree — xxv
Map of India and Pakistan, 1947 — xxvi
Map of Major Indian Cities — xxvii
Photographs follow page 66

1. EARLY LIFE — 3
2. MY MOTHER AND OUR FAMILY — 11
3. MY EDUCATION — 30
4. THE LAHORE CONGRESS, 1929 — 40
5. THE *SATYAGRAHA* MOVEMENT — 53
6. I AM ARRESTED, 1930 — 67
7. FIGHTING THE RAJ — 86
8. A NEW LIFE — 98
9. NEW DELHI AND SIMLA — 104
10. BOMBAY, 1942–47 — 117
11. WITH THE MINISTRY OF REHABILITATION, 1948–55 — 124
12. GENERAL ELECTIONS, 1952, 1957, AND 1971 — 135
13. WELFARE WORK AFTER PARTITION — 145

Epilogue — 157
Glossary — 159
Index — 161

Foreword

Manmohini Sahgal was born into one of the foremost families of India more than eight decades ago. The world was very different then from what it is now. And India was totally different. A colony of the United Kingdom, the jewel in the crown of the King Emperor, a part of the Empire on which the sun never set, India as it was seemed eternal.

The odds against the Empire's end and India's freedom and independence were tremendous. India was a large country but a poor one, for its economic resources had not been developed for the benefit of its inhabitants. Its population was diverse, with many religions and numerous languages, and India's government was continuously engaged in encouraging the frictions that arose from such diversity so that it could divide and rule. The people were unarmed, thus armed revolt was not an option for them. They were prevented, as far as was possible, from organizing for political purposes; any organization suspected of antigovernment activity was suppressed. How could such a country ever escape subordination to the most powerful empire the world had ever known?

Yet the determination of the people of India was such that they were not deterred from making the effort. In the peculiar conditions under which they lived, they rebelled through *satyagraha*, or nonviolent civil disobedience, the method they adopted under the leadership of Mahatma Gandhi. Since his battle against the revolting treatment of the blacks, colored, and Indians by the whites in South Africa, Gandhi had given much thought to the way in which India could regain her freedom. His ideas were influenced by Indian culture and by the writings of the great American philosopher, Henry Thoreau.

Though the struggle for independence was continuous, it had two peaks in its intensity—one in 1921 and the other in 1931. By the end of the latter year, the foundations of British rule in India had been so thoroughly shaken that the edifice could no longer stand. With the strains and stresses on the British economy and the British ethos caused by the Second World War, the building collapsed. For the first time in history, nonviolence had defeated the armed forces of a mighty empire.

In this long-lasting, nonviolent war, Manmohini's family played a leading role. Motilal Nehru, Jawaharlal Nehru, and Indira Gandhi are well known throughout the world. Less well known are other members of that illustrious family who were also part of the freedom struggle. They too suffered the consequences of opposition to foreign rule. They too went to jail, had their property confiscated, got beaten up and sometimes shot by the police, as did thousands of other Indians who fought for independence.

The story in this book is of an illustrious freedom fighter—of her trials and tribulations, her suffering, her joy in ultimate victory, and her pain with the partition of Pakistan. The fascinating tale here narrated is illustrative of the work, sacrifice, and dedication of hundreds of thousands of men and women who made the impossible possible. It is a story for all who are interested in human freedom.

B.K. Nehru
Indian Civil Service (retired),
Former Ambassador to the United States,
Former High Commissioner to Great Britain,
Former Governor of Assam,
Former Governor of Jammu and Kashmir,
Former Governor of Gujarat

Acknowledgments

The following individuals and institutions have played a role in bringing this book to its final production: Dr. Hari Dev Sharma, Deputy Director of the Nehru Memorial Museum and Library; Mr. Nazar H. Tiwana, Founder of the Organization for Universal Communal Harmony [TOUCH]; Anjali K. Varma, Advocate, Indian Supreme Court and High Court; Saloni N. Narang, novelist and short-story writer; Jim Ford, Photographer, State University of New York, Oswego; State University of New York Oswego, Faculty Enhancement Grant, Summer, 1993.

We would like to extend our heartfelt thanks to all for their help, guidance, and encouragement while we were working on this manuscript.

Manmohini Sahgal
Geraldine Forbes

Introduction

Manmohini Zutshi was born in the city of Allahabad, north India, in 1909. Although the British controlled this area of India, their dominion did not go unchallenged. For more than twenty-five years moderate Indian nationalists had asked for representative and responsible government. More militant nationalists demanded change and mobilized demonstrations of popular support for their position. Plans to partition the unwieldy province of Bengal touched off the *swadeshi* movement, which advocated both the boycott of foreign-made items and the rigorous support for domestically produced items. Increasingly the call was for *swaraj,* self-rule. When the government arrested militants, cells of revolutionaries began to plot violent acts. These "extremists" became the heroes who inspired young people throughout India.

In 1909 the British passed the Morley–Minto Reforms. This India Act of 1909 canceled the partition of Bengal, expanded the legislative councils, increased Indian representation, and introduced separate electorates for Muslims. Against the advice of the Indian National Congress, British legislators added a new dimension to Indian politics. From this time on, religious affiliation and political identity would be difficult to separate.

Manmohini was born in *Anand Bhavan* [Abode of Happiness], the mansion of Motilal Nehru. A successful lawyer at Allahabad High Court and a giant among the nationalist politicians of the time, Motilal

Nehru has been described as "a distinguished and wealthy barrister, modern, urbane, highly cultivated and lavishly generous."[1] Ladli Prasad Zutshi, Manmohini's father, was Motilal's nephew. When Motilal's elder sister Patrani (married to Lalji Prasad Zutshi) died, her infant son was sent to his maternal uncle's home. Motilal regarded Ladli Prasad as one of his own children, arranged his marriage to Lado Rani, and incorporated his nephew's family into the larger extended family.

The Nehrus were Brahmins from Kashmir who had settled in north India. A small, closely knit community, numbering between perhaps four thousand and five thousand in the 1920s, Kashmiri pandits pursued careers in law and government service. They have been called members of the "Urdu-speaking elite" who from the middle of the nineteenth century began to acquire knowledge of the English language.[2] Their caste associations were formed to react against restrictions that hindered secular progress.[3] While the Kashmiri pandits proceeded with their social reform agenda, they continued to support certain traditional customs that gave them a clear sense of identity. In other words, they were cosmopolitan, anxious to work with other communities, and interested in reform, but secure in their identities. For the *panditanis* [female members of this community], the caste associations discouraged child marriage and encouraged education. Traditionally, Kashmiri girls had received a rudimentary education for religious purposes and to keep household accounts, but their education was not the same as that designed for boys. Bombay, Bengal, and Madras led the way in providing formal education for girls and women. In contrast, north India was conservative, even backward. It was in north India that the sex ratio was lopsided, favoring men over women, and where female seclusion remained the model for respectable families whether Hindu or Muslim.

The men of the Nehru household were in the vanguard of Anglicization—speaking English; eating, dressing, and decorating their homes in the styles favored by the British; and sending their boys to the best English schools. Motilal's eldest child, Jawaharlal, was sent to England to study at Harrow and then Cambridge, while Vijayalakshmi and Krishna, his daughters, were taught by governesses from England. At the same time, Motilal's wife and her two widowed sisters formed a traditional block within their household. Undeterred, Motilal encouraged the younger women to participate in public activities. In 1909 Rameshwari (his niece-in-law) began the journal *Sri Darpan* [Mirror of Beauty], and in 1914 Rameshwari and Lado Rani (Ladli Prasad's wife and Manmohini's mother) joined the Allahabad Ladies' Branch of the Hindu Marriage Reform League. Not everyone in the community approved of the activities of the younger women of *Anand Bhavan,* but few openly criticized the wealthy and powerful Nehru family.

Manmohini was the third of four daughters born to Ladli Prasad and Lado Rani Zutshi. In 1910, after their last child was born, they moved to their own house in Allahabad. Like other progressive women of the era, Lado Rani had been encouraged to join "ladies' clubs" for companionship, discussion of public issues, and philanthropic activities. From their new home Lado Rani set up both a ladies' club and a girls' club, engaged a music teacher for her daughters, learned to ride a bicycle, and genuinely enjoyed her new experiments with personal freedom.

Lado Rani's daughters all grew to love learning, music, and travel. As they matured it became increasingly difficult to meet their intellectual needs with tutors, and so Lado Rani sought Motilal's permission to move with her daughters to Lahore. Lado Rani's widowed father lived in Lahore, but more important was the city's excellent missionary schools and patronage of music and the arts. Motilal agreed, and in 1917 Lado Rani and the girls moved to Lahore. Ladli Prasad remained in Allahabad, where he continued to practice law. That year the Secretary of State for India, Edwin Montagu, declared that the British Empire's goal for India was responsible government.

Mohandas K. Gandhi returned to India from South Africa in 1915. News of the protests he had organized electrified Indians, and Gandhi became the hero of the hour. Back in India, he established an ashram [colony] for his followers, courted arrest when he championed the cause of poor peasants in Champaran District of Bihar, and in 1918 supported a strike of textile workers in Ahmadabad.

At the conclusion of World War I the British passed another India Act, known as the Montagu–Chelmsford Reforms. Retaining a firm grip on their power over revenue and law and order, the British had increased responsible government only in the sense that they handed over nation-building subjects—health, education, public works, agriculture, and industry—to elected officials. Faced with demonstrations and demands for greater autonomy, the British enacted the repressive Rowlatt Bills in 1919. When Indians defied these restrictions on their freedom to organize and protest, they were massacred in the name of law and order.

In 1919 Motilal Nehru was President of the Indian National Congress at Amritsar, and Gandhi introduced *satyagraha* [truth force] as a guiding philosophy for protest. Mass support of both Hindus and Muslims could be organized by urging resistance to unjust laws. In addition, Gandhi envisioned a role for women in this nationalist struggle that promised to use only nonviolent techniques. From 1919 on, Gandhi was a guiding force in the Indian National Congress.

Manmohini was at this time an eleven-year-old schoolgirl. By her own account she only partially grasped what was happening but she was gaining a political education from her mother. Lado Rani tangled with missionary teachers over the extent to which her children would be introduced to Christianity and forced to respect imperial authority.

Her daughters learned their lessons well. Proud of their heritage, they became defiant and fearless young women. For anyone who holds fast to the stereotype of Indian women as sheltered, weak, and completely at the mercy of patriarchal forces, the ideas and deeds of Lado Rani Zutshi and her four daughters will come as something of a shock.

The inequities suffered by Indian women, viewed from a comparative perspective, seem no worse than those experienced by women in other societies. Child marriage, female seclusion, exclusion from important religious ceremonies, restrictions on inheritance and property ownership, strictures against remarriage, neglect of female education, mistreatment of widows and other women unprotected by males, and preference for male children were, unfortunately, experienced by women throughout the world. Some especially cruel practices, for example, *sati* (the requirement that women be burned alive on the funeral pyres of their dead husbands), were unique to India. However, *sati* was not widely practiced. Similarly, the harshness of the other customs varied from region to region and from community to community. In the nineteenth century, British missionaries and officials denounced Indians for both their gender ideology and their treatment of women. Certain that as Christians and Europeans their own gender relations were superior, these imperialists self-righteously declared the people they had conquered "unfit to rule." Furthermore, they argued, Indians would remain incapable of self-rule until their most intimate practices and customs had been modified to win foreign approval.

Well-intentioned Indian leaders sought to reform customs that they, in turn, condemned as accretions from the "dark age" (the pre-British period, sometimes identified with Muslim rule of India). Throughout the nineteenth century, Indian reformers tackled the practices that they and their British critics had identified as especially heinous: *sati*, female infanticide, prohibitions on remarriage for widows, strictures against educating females, dedication of females to temple service, and female seclusion. Largely untouched were cultural patterns shared by Indians and the British: the patriarchal family system, limitations on female inheritance, women's subordinate role in religion, lack of opportunity for gainful employment, and male control of female bodies. Nevertheless, in India there were some patriarchs who decided that the womenfolk of their families should be "liberated." In some cases this resulted in remarkable changes within a generation or two.

When Manmohini and her sisters pursued higher education (all four completed their bachelor's degrees, three completed their master's degrees) in the 1920s, they were among the first women of their community to do so. Daring to enter men's colleges marked them as rebels within a society still practicing sex segregation. For these young women, asserting one's right to think and act independently was truly part of "family culture."

Among Lado Rani's four daughters, Manmohini was the most rebellious. She was also a young woman with organizational and leadership skills. When protests against the British Raj began, her male colleagues asked her to lead them, and she did so boldly and without fear. During this period, from the late 1920s until the mid-1930s, Manmohini spoke publicly, organized protests, demonstrated, courted arrest, and was sentenced to prison on three separate occasions. Her dedication and commitment were unusual even for the most political of young women at the time. In fact, she consciously sought the British label "habitual offender." Her intensity reminds me of the women who joined revolutionary movements and engaged in violent protest.[4] Manmohini respected the revolutionaries and applauded their actions but rejected their invitations to join them. This was not how she intended to participate in the movement for India's freedom. As she made it clear to all around her, she supported Gandhiji and the concept of nonviolent struggle.

How can we understand Manmohini's social rebellion and political activism in a society that practiced sex segregation and looked askance at higher education for women? Historians who hold that class is the key to all that happens would point out she was a Kashmiri Brahmin. Others would stress family status, arguing that the Nehru women attained their positions because they belonged to this family. But these are generalizations, not answers. Belonging to an elite class does not guarantee political activism. Women of the Nehru family certainly learned about politics from an early age and were expected to support the freedom movement, but this does not explain why young men at Government College wanted Manmohini to be their leader. Furthermore, not all of the Nehru women actively participated in the freedom struggle. The answers have to be sought, I believe, in the notion of "family culture" and in Manmohini's personality.

Lado Rani's resettling of the family in Lahore may have irked some members of the family, but it was approved of by Motilal. Living as a family unit, Lado Rani and her four daughters were able to pursue education and music as well as bicycling, horseback riding, and a range of activities rarely engaged in by women. Manmohini's sister Janak became a teacher in 1930. Limitations were sometimes placed on the actions of these four women, but by and large their education, travel, and even defiance of authority were supported by the extended family. What these young women received from their families was more than support, however; their parents and extended family applauded what they did and backed them up with encouragement and financial resources.

In 1929 Manmohini was studying for her master's in history at Government College for Men in Lahore. Had the times been different, her fine intellect and love of learning would probably have propelled her toward teaching. But Manomohini had cut her teeth on politics, and when the situation called for a leader she emulated her mother and stepped into the fray. The young men who urged her forward and followed her directions must have recognized in her a special quality. According to her own description, she was quiet and unassuming, but at the same time she exuded competence and self-assurance. Mrs. Santosh Khanna, a friend in Delhi, said that her father remembers the stunning appearance of the four Zutshi sisters. Apparently these four young women, tall, attractive, and self-confident, turned heads wherever they went. Because Manmohini was a woman, female students were especially inspired and rushed forward to follow her example. When Manmohini was arrested, Janak left her position as a government servant, joined the protest, and courted arrest. Finally, Lado Rani Zutshi and three of her daughters were in prison at the same time.

Manmohini's description of prison life for women in north India is the finest that exists. Manmohini was imprisoned three times: in 1930, 1931, and 1932. From her memoirs we learn the details of prison life: the classification of prisoners as A, B, or C, depending on their status outside prison; the mundane existence of those incarcerated; and especially the day-to-day resistance in which they engaged. These chapters are extremely valuable for the insights they give us into the motivations of the women who engaged in such protest. This account is particularly important in shedding light on the debate over whether these women were acting of their own volition or were manipulated by Congress leaders.

There are many androcentric accounts of the Indian independence movement that focus on Gandhi's role in mobilizing women. On the opposite end of the spectrum are radical historians who have blamed Gandhi for sidetracking an impending feminist revolution. Still others, seeking tidy answers to the vexatious questions from the past, have assured us that the Indian National Congress, with the help of Gandhi, solved "the woman question."

These pat answers are unsatisfactory when we talk with and read the actual accounts of women who were involved in this movement. Years ago Helena Dutt (a Bengali revolutionary) said, "We were like caged tigers," referring to herself and other young women who were politically active in the early 1930s. She did not use the "bird in a gilded cage" imagery that we find in the literature of the nineteenth century. Instead, she spoke of women as powerful tigers ready to spring into action when liberated. Education was the key to unlocking the cage. Manmohini's memoirs are another version of the role that women played as revolutionaries by their own conviction.

When Gandhi called a halt to the *satyagraha* movement and urged his followers to concentrate on constructive work, Manmohini decided to become the Principal of a Congress school. In 1935 she traveled to the province of Bihar to take charge of the Bihar *Mahila Vidyapith* [Bihar Female School] for fifteen- and sixteen-year-old village girls. It is significant, I believe, that in her few months at this school she received more criticism from the Indian community than she had during her years of fighting the British. As a political leader, she received almost unanimous approval. Traditional families allowed their daughters to follow her to prison; *tonga* [horse-drawn passenger cart] drivers stood their ground to protect her; even her jailors admired her spirit. But when she went to Bihar, there were no British to fight and no young male students to take up the cudgels on her behalf. There was only a poorly financed school in a district of conservative people. Some of the changes she attempted, for example, shoes for girls, had to be abandoned. She stuck by her decision to introduce physical fitness classes, yet compromised with the opposition by holding them in a secluded place.

In 1935 Manmohini married Amrit Lal Sahgal, a chartered accountant and a Punjabi. The bride and groom belonged to different communities. It was a "love marriage"; Manmohini was twenty-six years old. Her granddaughter repeats a favorite family story that Amrit Sahgal used to play the violin under Manmohini's jail window. Whenever he made this claim, Manmohini would remind him that her cell did not have a window and if he serenaded anyone, it must have been the warden. As a married woman Manmohini moved to Delhi and then to Bombay, bore three children (a boy and two girls), became absorbed with the details of running a middle-class household, and resumed the social work she was introduced to as a child. From Delhi she made the annual pilgrimage to Simla for six months, and, just when this was declared unnecessary, her husband was transferred to Bombay. With her children enrolled in school, Manmohini decided to work toward her Ph.D. in history. At the end of the war her husband was again transferred to Delhi, making it impossible for her to complete her degree. These were years of "constructive work," as Gandhi called it. Many worked for social uplift, others worked for laws to bring India into conformity with the "civilized world" as defined by the International Labor Organization, League of Nations, and other international bodies, and still others worked to develop institutions that would bring about social change.

When the family returned to Delhi in 1947, the British were leaving and the country had been newly divided into India and Pakistan. The object of this division was to save lives and prevent bloodshed, but, unfortunately, the exchange of populations was accompanied by murderous attacks on refugees, the abduction of women, and, finally, large camps of displaced persons. Manmohini became involved in refugee work as a volunteer and was soon asked to take on major responsibilities. The tasks she was assigned were worthy of the attention of a skilled bureaucrat, but she always worked as a volunteer with a token salary of one rupee per month. In the eastern state of West Bengal, Chief Minister Dr. B.C. Roy appointed Renuka Ray, a woman who did similar work, to the position of Minister of Refugees and Rehabilitation.

In 1952 Manmohini was persuaded to run for election to the Lok Sabha, the lower house of the Indian legislative branch of government. As she has recounted, this was a charade from the very start. Nominally committed to having women elected, party officials used their power to allocate seats to serve other interests. Because women did not form a recognizable constituency, there was no need to satisfy their demands. Nor was Manmohini helped by her cousin Jawaharlal Nehru, India's first Prime Minister. He supported her candidacy but he would not interfere. Other forays into political life were equally unsettling. Manmohini had been a formidable leader during the struggle for political independence, but, after this victory, Congress leaders had no need for her services. From her account of those exciting years of political activism it becomes apparent that she was a leader from the ranks, not someone handpicked by the leaders of Congress committees. In times of agitation, they were forced to work with her, but when it was their turn to call the shots, Manmohini was not on their list of approved women.

Shut out from one path for political action, Manmohini turned to other causes. She became involved with organized labor, fighting the battles of the underdog, and with women's organizations. Her concerns and the numbers of organizations she worked with were many. The hallmark of her work is attention to detail, unflagging energy, persistence and commitment. Power corrupts, she insists. This is a truism, she maintains, that in her experience is constantly being reconfirmed. She finds social service preferable because it calls forth dedication and can bring results. But her efforts are not casual volunteerism; for Manmohini social service is a full-time career. At age eighty-four, as President of the Indian Council of Social Welfare in New Delhi, Manmohini regards her major project as the building of a working women's hostel in New Delhi. She has been the general supervisor of this project, working with others to secure the funding, buy the land, and collect bids for construction. The expected date for completion is 1995.

Manmohini's political ambitions were not similarly rewarded, and, like so many women of her generation, she feels betrayed. The Indian National Congress, and particularly Gandhi, had promised that women's issues would be taken seriously in independent India. But women were thwarted in their efforts to enter the legislatures and were relegated to the position of helpmates. These women were told that they did not understand politics, they lacked the necessary connections, and they would not be able to win elections. But these assumptions were never tested. The assertion of party bosses that most women could not be elected was accepted by the rank and file in the party, who, in the final analysis, were more comfortable with women as political petitioners.

Manmohini had been raised in a sex-segregated environment, but she defied the rules to attend a men's college and won the approval of the men with whom she worked. She inspired both women and men with her bold defiance of the British. In leading demonstrations and in prison she exhibited a special understanding of women's condition, and she displayed these sympathies later when working with refugee women. But she refused to be categorized as a leader of women only. During her lifetime of work she has exhibited as much empathy for men as for women. If I were to categorize her it would be as a humanist with special sympathy for women's condition.

I met Manmohini by accident. In 1988 I received a phone call from Nazar Tiwana in Chicago telling me he was certain I would want to meet his aunt. He had heard from a professor at the University of Chicago that I was interested in Indian women activists from the 1930s. A few weeks later I spoke to Manmohini Sahgal on the phone. As we talked, names, places, and dates began to fit together and I suddenly became aware that I was talking with one of "the Zutshi women." I knew a great deal about the exploits of "Mrs. Zutshi and her four daughters," but, as has been the case with many of the women I have read about in official accounts, marriage brought about a change of name, making it difficult to draw the connection. In addition, one of the few books on women in the freedom movement listed Manmohini Zutshi Sahgal as deceased.

A few weeks after this phone call, I drove to Toronto to meet Manmohini. It was an extraordinary encounter, and I left with a taped interview and voluminous notes on the demonstrations in north India. Manmohini told me at the time that her memoirs had been promised to an Indian publisher. When I was in Delhi in 1989, I read a draft of her memoirs and became interested in Manmohini's girlhood. A few months later it became apparent that the original plans to publish her memoirs would not work out and she agreed to let me edit an American edition. In 1991 Manmohini stayed with me when she was visiting the United States. By then we were beginning to edit the manuscript. At age eighty-two Manmohini lectured to my students and captivated a classroom full of young people who had accepted the American media stereotype of Indian women as oppressed and devoid of any agency.

Since that time, Manmohini and I have exchanged a bundle of letters and chapters and pieces of chapters as we worked together on editing, rewriting, and extending the manuscript to prepare it for publication in the Foremother Legacies series. It has been a great pleasure for me to work with the memoirs of another historian. As a South Asian historian, I have been excited about finding a detailed memoir of a female freedom fighter. As a professor who teaches women's studies, I am delighted to be able to add another feminine voice to our record of this period of Indian history. This book also adds to our understanding of gender construction and the maintenance of gender differences. Significantly, we can begin to understand how the British defined Indians as rigidly adhering to sex segregation and then scrupulously upheld this cultural pattern. I believe this narrative also adds to our understanding of the "feminist movement" in India. Manmohini was not a feminist in a European sense, but her concern with women's well-being and women's rights causes us to doubt the utility of trying to apply Western standards in other cultures.

Manmohini has been a foremother to me. She has had an interesting life, and her service to humanity has been considerable. Despite her extraordinary talent for politics, she was shut out of a political career. The Foremother Legacies series was designed to allow us to hear the "voices" of women who have led inspiring lives. I hope that Manmohini's memoir will continue to inspire. I know she has been a genuine inspiration to her granddaughter Chanda Narang. When she was a first-year college student in a composition course, Chanda wrote about her grandmother as President of the Child Welfare Association. At that time Manmohini was controlling a budget of about five million rupees. "It couldn't be in better hands," Chanda wrote. "She is honest, uncorruptable, scrupulous, abrasive, aggressive and the most terrible P.R.O. [Public Relations Officer] I've ever met. I've heard her say so often, 'Absolutely not, I'm not going to allow it, it's illegal and I don't care whose orders they are. . . .' She can be very formal, forbidding, straightforward, and obstinate. But she is also brave, honest, kind and frank. She never complains. She just carries on living by her principles, fighting for the causes she believes in."[5]

Geraldine Forbes
New Delhi, 1993

Notes

1. Michael Brecher, *Nehru: A Political Biography* (Boston: Beacon Press, 1959), p. 1.
2. Kusum Pant, *The Kashmiri Pandit: Story of a Community in Exile in the Nineteenth and Twentieth Centuries* (New Delhi: Allied Publishers, 1987), pp. viii, 99–105.
3. Ibid., p. 141.
4. Geraldine Forbes, "Goddesses or Rebels? The Women Revolutionaries of Bengal," *The Oracle* 2, no. 2 (April 1980): 1–15; Titha Mandal, *Women Revolutionaries of Bengal, 1905–1939* (Calcutta: Minerva Associates, 1991).
5. Chanda Narang, paper for Freshman English, Mills College, Oakland, California, Spring 1984.

The Nehru Family Tree

Gangadhar Nehru *m.* Indrani

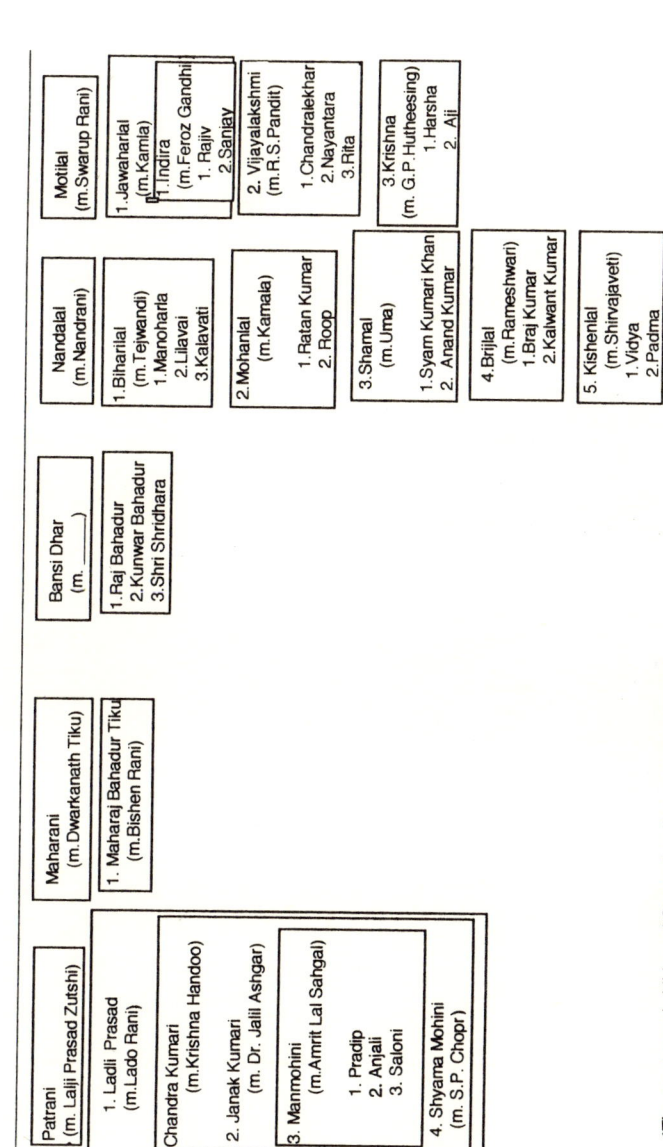

Patrani
(m. Lalji Prasad Zutshi)

1. Ladli Prasad
   (m. Lado Rani)
2. Chandra Kumari
   (m. Krishna Handoo)
3. Janak Kumari
   (m. Dr. Jalil Asngar)
4. Manmohini
   (m. Amrit Lal Sahgal)
   1. Pradip
   2. Anjali
   3. Saloni
5. Shyama Mohini
   (m. S.P. Chopr)

Maharani
(m. Dwarkanath Tiku)

1. Maharaj Bahadur Tiku
   (m. Bishen Rani)

Bansi Dhar
(m. ____)

1. Raj Bahadur
2. Kunwar Bahadur
3. Shri Shridhara

Motilal
(m. Swarup Rani)

1. Jawaharlal
   (m. Kamla)
   1. Indira
      (m. Feroz Gandhi)
      1. Rajiv
      2. Sanjay
2. Vijayalakshmi
   (m. R.S. Pandit)
   1. Chandralekha
   2. Nayantara
   3. Rita
3. Krishna
   (m. G.P. Hutheesing)
   1. Harsha
   2. Aji

Nandalal
(m. Nandrani)

1. Biharilal
   (m. Tejwandi)
   1. Manoharla
   2. Lilavai
   3. Kalavati
2. Mohanlal
   (m. Kamala)
   1. Ratan Kumar
   2. Roop
3. Shamal
   (m. Uma)
   1. Syam Kumari Khan
   2. Anand Kumar
4. Brijlal
   (m. Rameshwari)
   1. Braj Kumar
   2. Kalwant Kumar
5. Kishenlal
   (m. Shirvajaveti)
   1. Vidya
   2. Padma

*The great grand-children of Gangadhar Nehru are not all listed.

INDIA AND PAKISTAN - 1947

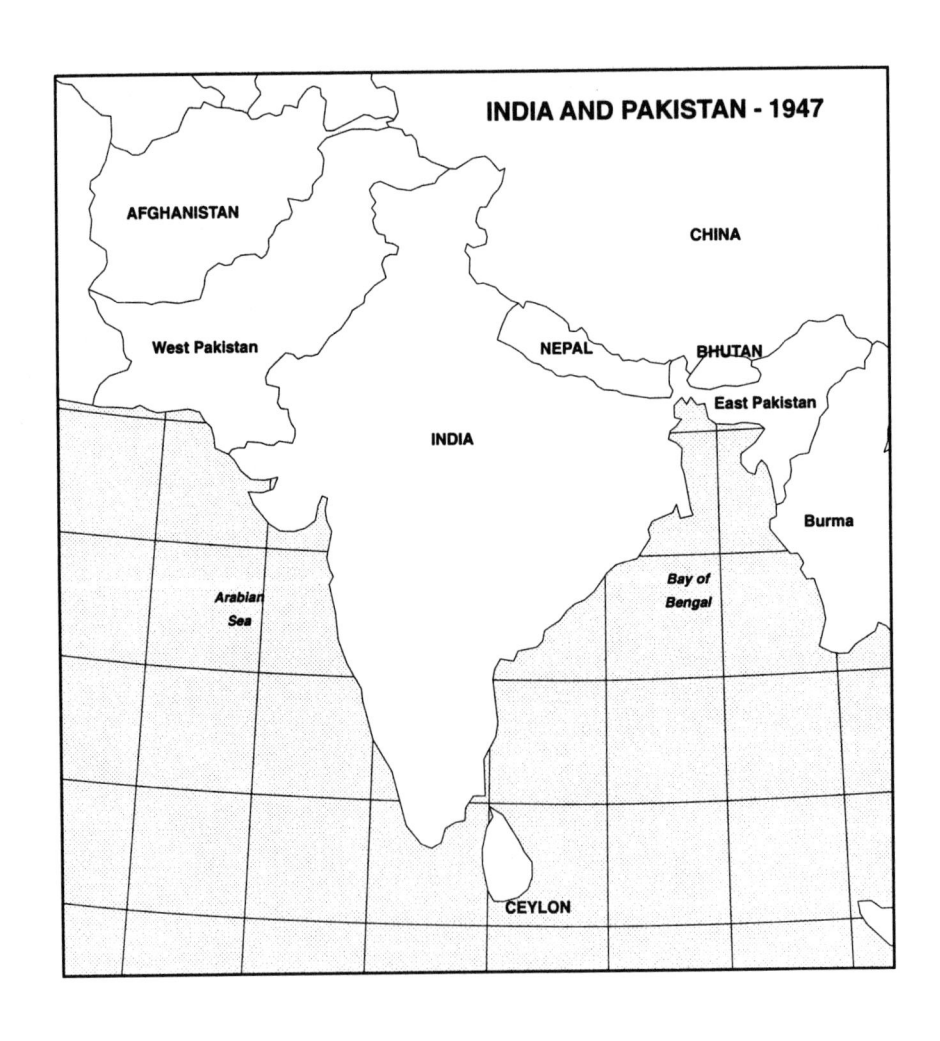

MAJOR INDIAN CITIES

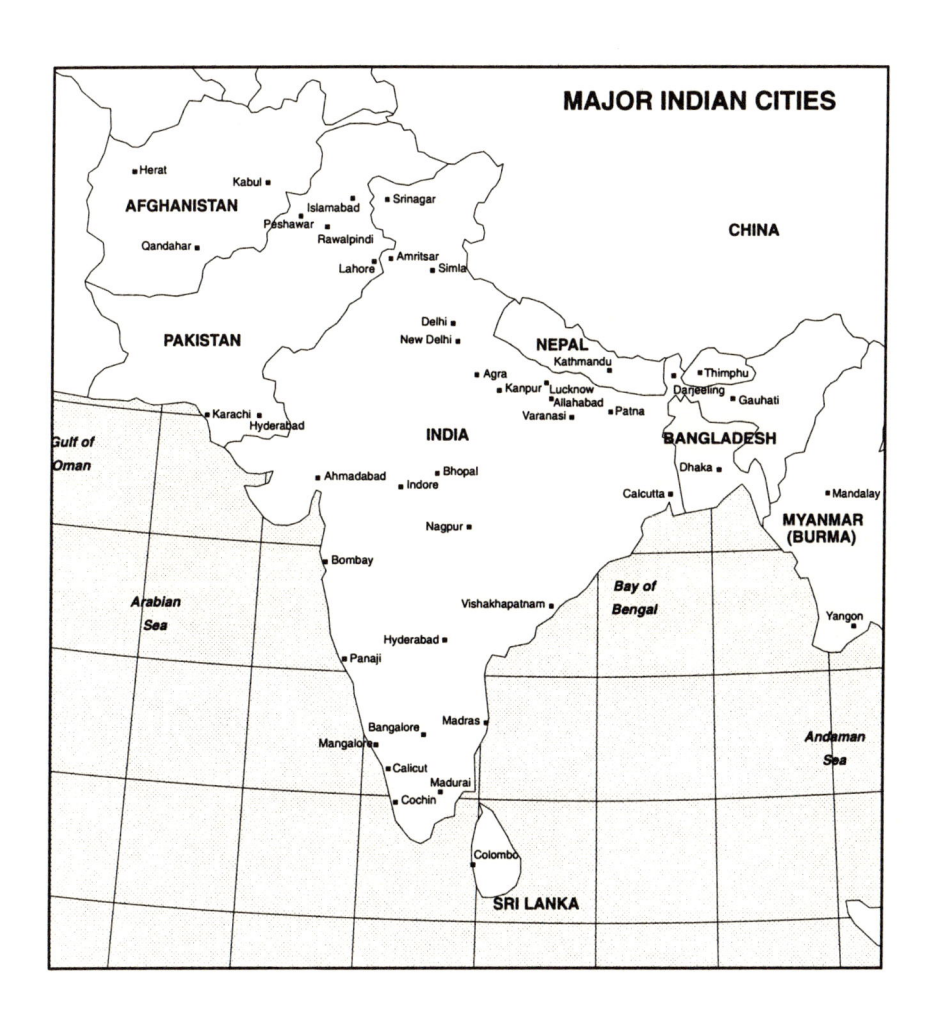

Manmohini Zutshi Sahgal

An Indian Freedom Fighter Recalls Her Life

1

Early Life

I was born in Allahabad in *Anand Bhavan* [Abode of Happiness], now known as *Swaraj Bhavan* [Freedom House], which was gifted to the nation in the 1930s by its owner, Pandit Motilal Nehru.

My father, the late Pandit Ladli Prasad Zutshi, was Pandit Motilal's sister's son. Left motherless at the tender age of three months, he was first brought up by his maternal grandmother, as was the custom, and then by his uncle Motilal. My father was not the only nephew in the family to be cared for by his uncle. Motilal's own father, Gangadhar Nehru, passed away before Motilal was born, so Motilal was looked after by his elder brother Nandalal, sixteen years his senior. Nandalal had five sons and one daughter. His two elder sons, Biharilal and Mohanlal, both advocates, were already on their own. When Nandalal died, his widow, with the rest of their family, came to live with Motilal. Mohanlal was an exceptional man, dedicated to social work from his early days. He had great organizing ability and wore *swadeshi* [made in the country] clothing long before Gandhiji advocated it. I remember visiting *swadeshi* fairs that he organized in Allahabad.

Motilal's father, Gangadhar Nehru, had settled in Delhi as *kotwal* in the court of the last Mughal Emperor Bahadur Shah Zafar. The *kotwal* in those days was a very important official in charge of law and order for the whole city—more like the Chief Commissioner in modern times. A photograph of Gangadhar dressed in the full regalia of his office can be seen in the Nehru Museum in New Delhi.

Motilal's mother, Indrani (known as Jiyo Maji) was a remarkable woman. She reared her family in the traditional pattern and was respected and admired by the Kashmiri community. She taught herself to read Hindi and later on learned Persian by sitting in on her sons' lessons. She had three sons and two daughters. Her daughters, both with very unusual names, Patrani and Maharani, died young, each leaving one son. Patrani was the mother of my father, Ladli Prasad Zutshi. The family lived in Agra, where the eldest son, Nandalal, had a flourishing practice. It was Motilal who moved the family to Allahabad, where he practiced at the High Court.

Motilal was a patriarch in the true sense of the word. He sheltered a number of nieces and nephews in his large house, *Anand Bhavan*. His lucrative practice at the bar made it possible for him to look after such a large family. Otherwise, I do not think it would have been possible to feed, clothe, and educate so many young people. We all looked upon him as the head of the family, and he was the only paternal grandfather that we knew. In fact, it was at his suggestion that we called him *Dadaji* [paternal grandfather], even though his own son Jawaharlal had not yet married. I remember very well the old *Anand Bhavan* when the whole family used to live there. The house was big enough to accommodate the whole family and it hummed with activity.

I do not know who was responsible for housekeeping. To feed such a large family must have been a chore in itself. I have been told that the milk, which came in large quantities, was boiled in the presence of Mrs. Motilal Nehru or under the supervision of her personal servant, Mithai. It was then divided into two containers and distributed to all the daughters-in-law and nephews in their respective rooms. My mother recounted that broken rice used to be collected from the store room, and it was the duty of the daughters-in-law of the house to separate the full grains from the broken ones. I suppose her daughters-in-law used to respond to her call to do this work, but my mother never joined them. For this she naturally came in for a lot of criticism. Even the afternoon snacks for the family were regulated. One *anna* [one-sixteenth of a rupee] was allocated for snacks for each male member of the family and two *pice* [one-sixty-fourth of a rupee] for each of their wives.

I have no recollection of my own grandfather, Lalji Prasad Zutshi. After the death of his wife, he never remarried. He lived in Gwalior.

For some reason he had no contact with his only child, Ladli Prasad, until the latter was old enough to be married. Then Lalji Prasad arranged his son's engagement. Motilal protested that Lalji Prasad could not suddenly claim a father's privilege after he had taken no notice while his son was growing up. It was Motilal who had looked after young Ladli Prasad since his birth; therefore, he claimed, the engagement to Lado Rani arranged by him should stand. Lalji Prasad was so incensed that he did not attend the wedding and broke off all connections with his son.

Ladli Prasad had no further contact with his father. Of course, the fact that he had four daughters and no son did not endear him to his own father. I am the third among my sisters, and we were all born at *Anand Bhavan*. I remember Mother telling us that after asking the permission of Motilal, she wrote to her father-in-law seeking permission to visit him. The old man never replied. The only contact my father had with this side of his family was when my grandfather passed away and Father went to Gwalior to settle his affairs. It was then that he met the rest of his family.

My mother, Lado Rani, was a woman with radical ideas for her time. She was the only child of her father, Jeevan Lal Tikku, and had lost her mother when she was only four years old. She was brought up by her father's sister, Mrs. Bishan Narain Razdan, who had four sons and two daughters of her own. Although my mother had no formal education, she studied Urdu and Hindi with her cousins and was fluent in both languages. Because her aunt had progressive views, no inhibitions were placed on young Lado, who even played cricket with her male cousins. She was raised with a great deal of freedom until, at age fifteen, she was married to my father, who was then studying law. After qualifying, Father began practicing at the Lahore High Court of Allahabad.

Lado Rani came from a more or less traditional Kashmiri family and suddenly found herself faced with the modern way of life as practiced in Motilal's household. She not only had to learn English to be able to converse with the wives of British officials who occasionally visited Indian families, but also had to dress impeccably with shoes and stockings and be able to use a knife and fork. These days this seems easy, but think of those times! Women who had never stepped out of their homes suddenly had a family that flouted conventions and made up new ones to suit the occasion. Lado Rani quickly adapted to this new way of life. She started taking English and art lessons and actually became a very good artist; she even painted her own sari borders. I have one of her oil paintings in my sitting room.

Motilal was a reformer and a leader. He ran two kitchens in his house—one for Indian food and the other for European food. For the latter he had a Muslim cook and bearers. Naturally, there were two dining rooms—one fully equipped in the Western style, with tables and chairs, and the other, the Indian dining room, furnished with marble flooring where the family sat on small *asans* [individual mats] and ate off silver *thalis* [plates] placed on separate little tables. Mrs. Motilal was orthodox. I doubt if she had ever had Western food in her own home although she had been abroad.

There was a swimming pool in the house where the younger generation, both men and women, could have a dip even if they could not swim. My mother recounted an incident when one of the women lost her gold ring in the pool. Jawaharlal, an excellent swimmer, was asked to dive in and get it out. How he teased his sisters-in-law! They had to beg and plead with him before he actually retrieved the ring.

Another instance of Motilal's progressive ideas was the way he treated his Muslim *munshi* [legal assistant], Mubarak Ali. Mubarak Ali lived in a cottage in the same compound. Manzar Ali, Mubarak Ali's son, had free run of the house and was treated like a member of the family. This boy called all his older "cousins," like my father, *bhai* [brother] and their wives, *bhabi* [sister-in-law]. We called him Manna *Bhai* and looked on him as another uncle. In fact, it is said that Manzar Ali never married because he could not find a girl in his community who was as educated and as progressive as his so-called sisters-in-law. Those were the days when most educated men holding high office were so orthodox that they used to bathe and change clothes if they came in contact with a British officer or a low-caste Hindu. Even my husband's paternal grandfather, Rai Bahadur Boota Mal, the first Indian sessions judge of the High Court of Lahore, used to do so.

It was only after the birth of my younger sister Shyama in September 1910 that we moved out of *Anand Bhavan* to our own house on three acres of land at 23 Hamilton Road in Allahabad. This area had been developed when King George V came to the throne in England, and so it was named "George Town." My father was very fond of gardening, so he planted a variety of fruit trees in the compound. I remember the huge mango tree on our back lawn where my mother used to hold meetings of her *mahila sammelan* [ladies' association].

Father had a rose garden as well, which he used to tend himself, even though we had a full-time gardener with two assistants. Other improvements Father made included a tube well, installed in the compound so there was never any shortage of water. The house was typical of the architecture of those days: large rooms, high ceilings designed to keep the house cool, and deep front and back verandahs running the length of the house. There was a huge terrace as well, where the family gathered mornings and evenings in early summer. I do not remember if the "drawing room," furnished in the Western style with sofa sets, was ever used.

In all Kashmiri households there was one room—the main sitting room—with wooden platforms that could be moved around individually or joined together. These were covered with thick mattresses and white sheets, and there were large bolsters to lean on. Anyone visiting the family used to either sit on this *takhtposh* in the Indian fashion or sit on the few chairs scattered here and there in the room. The *takhtposh* could be used for an afternoon siesta, for reading, or for sewing. No visitor was considered so formal that the "drawing room" had to be opened. Kashmiri families also had a *pan-dan* [*pan* box], placed on a separate table. *Pan* [betel-leaf rolled with spices] was offered to guests as an act of courtesy. It could never be overlooked. My father developed a habit of chewing *pan*, so he kept his *pan-dan* separate from the one for general use. A parcel of the particular variety of *pan* leaves that he favored was forwarded to him whenever he left Allahabad or came to visit any of his daughters.

One room of the house was always kept locked, as it contained the wardrobes of the entire family and other odds and ends. This practice was followed by my mother after we moved to Lahore even though our houses were not that large.

As was the custom in respectable Indian families in those days, none of my sisters nor any of my female cousins were sent to school. Motilal had a resident governess for his two daughters, and the rest of the family followed suit by having day-governesses who would come to the house to teach the girls. I was the first girl in our family to be sent to school, and I went at the age of seven years. I was admitted to St. Mary's Convent in Allahabad, but, being a very sickly child and greatly attached to my mother, I hated going to school and used to weep copiously every day.

I remember vaguely Jawaharlal's wedding in Delhi in February

1916. The *barat* [bridegroom's party] left by special train from Allahabad. Firecrackers were placed under the engine, and, as the train moved out of the station, they exploded with a loud noise, much to the excitement of us children. We have a group photograph of the Nehru family with their guests holding a banner that reads: "Nehru Wedding Camp." Years later I asked my father to point out the exact building where the *barat* stayed in Delhi. He indicated Ludlow Castle, a building on the crossing of Alipur Road (now Sham Nath Marg) and Raj Niwas Road in old Delhi. This has since been demolished, and in its place stands the Model School for Boys.

In the Kashmiri community there is a *puja* [act of worship] called *pushpa puja* held after the marriage ceremony before the bride leaves for her husband's home. It invokes the blessings of the gods on the young married couple while the groom's and bride's parents and other elders shower flowers on them. The mantras [sacred verses] are sung by the pandits [priests], who are generally out of tune. So, for Jawaharlal's wedding, Pandit Motilal had us—all the girls of his family—trained in singing the mantras. The mantras had been put to music by our music master in Allahabad, who accompanied the *barat* to Delhi. Since the wedding was on *basant panchami* day [celebration for the coming of spring], all of us wore yellow silk saris and carried baskets of flowers lined with yellow silk. It looked very picturesque and was the first time in any Kashmiri wedding that the pandits had to take a back seat and the invocations were sung by a group of young girls. Anything new started by Motilal became the fashion immediately.

Our lives in Allahabad were also marked by reform. There was a ladies' club in Allahabad patronized by the wives of British officers stationed in Allahabad; the commissioner's wife was its President. The atmosphere of this club was very formal and stilted. My mother, Lado Rani, decided to organize another women's club, which she called *mahila sammelan* [ladies' association]. It met once a month and was composed of Indian women who felt at ease with one another. Lado Rani had organized this club with her friend Mrs. Shanta Banerjea, the wife of R.N. Banerjea, a neighbor and an advocate.

Lado Rani also felt that the daughters of these women needed some sort of recreation. She had four daughters of her own, so she organized a *kumari sabha* [girls' club] for them to meet, stage plays, and generally have a good time. I have a hazy recollection of my eldest sister

Chandra teaching my younger sister Shyama and myself some nursery rhyme in Hindi which we had to recite somewhere. The girls were not permitted to go to the "bioscope," as the cinema was called, so the *kumari sabha* was a boon for us.

Lado Rani also wanted her girls to learn music, but this was unheard of in those days. Only girls of dubious character learned singing. Lado Rani broke with this tradition and engaged a music teacher, who was called *Ustadji* [Mr. Music Master], to teach her two older daughters, Chandra and Janak, to sing. The music teacher was ordered to come in the middle of the afternoon when the men were at work and most women were having their siesta. He was also instructed to sing softly so that the neighbors would not hear. I suppose he was looking for other students, so he paid no heed to this advice. The neighbors were not deaf, and the lady living to the left of our house, a busybody who was fond of gossip, once asked Mother whether she had a music master for her girls because she had heard singing in the afternoons. Lado Rani did not have the courage to tell her to mind her own business, so she suggested that perhaps the lady had been dreaming!

Realizing that in Allahabad, under such restrictions, she would not be able to give her daughters the education she desired, Lado Rani sought Motilal's permission to move to Lahore in the Punjab, where her own father lived. The Punjab was reputed to be more progressive as far as women's education was concerned. Motilal gave his permission, and all of us, except for my father, moved to Lahore in 1917.

Mother left the four of us with her aunt in Amritsar while she went to Lahore to select a school for us and to look for suitable accommodations. She went first to the Jesus and Mary Convent where Indian girls of good families went, but were not allowed to mix with Anglo-Indian girls. The school had an Indian section with its own staff, and the Indian girls had a separate playground. Lado Rani rejected this institution out of hand. The second school on her list was Queen Mary's College, more or less a finishing school for Indian girls whose parents did not desire higher education for their children. Although it catered to Indians only, the girls were selected from families who had proved their loyalty to the British crown. The first question the principal asked Mother was whether my father had been rewarded by "the Crown." Was he a recipient of some title or award? My mother answered in the negative, but the principal condescendingly agreed to admit all four of us as a special case.

Mother was so disgusted that she left. Finally, she found the Sacred Heart Convent, run by the Belgian Sisters of Charity exclusively for Indian girls. The Belgian Sisters were unconcerned with honors and loyalty to the British Government, and so our schooling in Lahore began at Sacred Heart Convent. Little did we imagine what far-reaching effects this would have on our lives or that we would be involved in the freedom struggle many years later. Life in the Sacred Heart Convent was not free from problems for us. Since Mother was a woman with a forceful personality and strong views, she often clashed with the school authorities over little things. Looking back now, some of these seem so trivial that I am surprised that a woman of such progressive and broadminded views could be so narrowminded at times. Once, for example, my elder sister Janak was asked by her sewing teacher to bring material to school, as the class was to be taught to cut and sew nightdresses. Mother promptly put her foot down, remarking that since her daughters did not wear nightdresses there was no need for them to learn to sew them.

So long as the Mother Superior was there—a very gentle, understanding, and persuasive lady—an open clash was avoided. But there came a time when the Reverend Mother was transferred and her successor, Sister Mary, assumed the full powers and duties of the Mother Superior. Sister Mary was a woman with a personality as forceful as my mother's, and she would not tolerate anything that would undermine her authority as head of the institution. Clashes between her and Mother assumed such colossal proportions that there came a time when we had to leave the school. But more on this later.

2

My Mother and Our Family

My mother, Lado Rani Zutshi, settled in Lahore in 1917 to educate her daughters. She had a great deal of influence on me, and as I grew older I assisted her in many projects. As soon as she was settled in Lahore she joined the YWCA to continue her English and painting lessons. In the evenings she bicycled to her classes. No other Indian lady of her status in Lahore had the courage to do this. The only concession she made to society's rules was to have her own servant running behind her bicycle so that in case of accident she would not have to ask for help from a stranger; her servant would be there to help her. Fortunately for all concerned, such an occasion never arose. As she got more and more involved in public work and the demands of family, she gave up her lessons at the YWCA.

In Lahore, she started a ladies' recreation club and became its president. The club met in Ratan Bagh, a garden with very high walls that was eminently suited for this purpose. The secretary of the club was her dear friend Marzia Rashid, wife of Justice Abdul Rashid, who retired as Chief Justice of the Punjab High Court after the partition of the country. The club was patronized by "society ladies" and was extremely popular. Much of the credit for this should be given to the owner of Ratan Bagh, Dewan Kishan Kishore, a multimillionaire of Lahore and an extremely orthodox man. The ladies of his family lived in very strict *purdah* [seclusion], and his sons, although products of the

Government College for Men in Lahore, always dressed in "traditional" clothing, that is, the Mughal/Hindu *angarkha* [long jacket worn by men in north India] and turbans. It was a big step for Dewan Kishan Kishore to permit women to play badminton and sit and chat in his garden.

Mother also started a *kumari sabha* for her daughters and their friends. It had the same aims and objectives as the one she had started in Allahabad. In 1918, the *kumari sabha* was rehearsing a play about Mother India in deep slumber and the efforts of her children to rouse her. (I have forgotten the title, but it was written in Hindi by the famous playwright Bharatendu Harish Chandra.) The rehearsals were in full swing and the date was set for the final show when Gandhiji, who had returned from South Africa and was fast becoming a thorn in the side of the British Government, was arrested and sentenced to six years' imprisonment. The news of his arrest was sufficient for Mother to cancel the play. As it happened, it was never rescheduled. Then followed the atrocities of the Jallianwala *Bagh* at Amritsar and the order to impose martial law in the Punjab.

In 1917 we were enrolled in Sacred Heart Convent School in Lahore. The times we were living in were such that Indians were constantly being humiliated and terrorized. For example, in Champaran District of Bihar, European planters decided that indigo would be a profitable crop. They took lands on contract from the government, and, although farmers were not in favor of growing indigo, they were forced to do so. Those who refused were beaten up and had their cattle impounded and their houses looted. Recourse to a court of law was not easy, and, in any case, the courts were controlled by the European planters. The planters also levied several unauthorized taxes.

In short, the lives of the farmers were worse than those of serfs. On hearing of the injustice to the poor farmers of Champaran District, Gandhi urged the government to institute an inquiry. As a result, the planters were asked to refund the portions of their exactions that the Inquiry Commission considered unlawful.

Gandhiji's attention was also drawn to the famine in Gujarat, particularly in Kheda District. The farmers, unable to pay land revenue, had asked the government to waive their taxes as a relief measure. The authorities turned down their request. Gandhiji was approached by the farmers' leaders, and he advised them not to pay this tax, thereby launching his noncooperation movement. The government confiscated the farmers' property and cattle, leaving them completely impoverished.

Considering this agitation of the farmers a conspiracy, the government appointed a commission under the chairmanship of Sir F.A. Rowlatt in December 1917. Its task was to investigate and report on the nature and criminal conspiracies of the revolutionary movement in India. The commission was purportedly to deal with the revolutionaries only, but in fact it was commissioned to deal with all political agitation, whether revolutionary or constitutional.

The Rowlatt Bills of 1919 included both preventive and punitive measures. Preventive measures included restricting suspects to their residences, requiring suspects to report periodically to the police, and allowed for arrest and detention without cause. Punitive measures included trying seditious crimes by a judicial bench consisting of three judges without jury, preliminary commitment proceedings, or appeal.

The government wanted to have the bills enacting these measures passed during the February 1919 session of the Imperial Legislative Council. In vain, Gandhiji protested that with the Defense of India Act already in force these bills would be redundant. However, they were passed in March 1919 and came to be known as the Rowlatt Act. When Gandhiji realized that these measures would be passed, he organized a nationwide resistence campaign. He called on the Indian people to hold and observe a countrywide *hartal* [a morally inspired strike] on April 6, 1919. As a result, Gandhiji was arrested on his way to Delhi and Amritsar but was set free in Bombay. The *hartal* was observed peacefully in Lahore, Amritsar, and other places.

On April 13, 1919, the Amritsar Congress decided to hold a meeting to protest the Rowlatt Bills in an enclosed area in the heart of the city known as Jallianwala *Bagh*. This "garden," or open space, was surrounded by tall houses and had only one entrance. About twenty thousand people had gathered there for the protest meeting when the Amritsar Martial Law Commander, General R.E. Dyer, accompanied by fifty soldiers armed with rifles, arrived, ordered immediate dispersal, and then ordered his troops to open fire. The troops fired 1,650 rounds of ammunition directly into the crowd for ten minutes. The meeting had been peaceful throughout. Why a high official like General Dyer arrived and ordered this action is difficult to explain.

When the firing began, people ran helter-skelter to save themselves. Many died and many more fell into an uncovered well. Under Dyer's orders, the wounded were left in the Jallianwala *Bagh* all night without water or medical aid. General Dyer is supposed to have said that "his purpose was to strike terror into the whole of the Punjab." Martial law was declared all over the province. Motor cars, horse carriages, and even bicycles were confiscated. People were whipped and made to crawl on their stomachs. As I recall, martial law commissioners tried 298 people on major charges and sentenced 51 to death (later some of these sentences were commuted), 46 to be transported for life, and 115 to various terms of imprisonment. One of my maternal uncles was arrested at this time. He was a peace-loving man, a musician who had never taken part in political activities.

Lawyers and their solicitors were ordered to get themselves registered with the police and to not leave the city without permission. No more than two persons were permitted to walk together. Students had to report to the police four times daily at locations several miles from their educational institutions. Martial law notices were pasted on the walls of buildings, and the occupants were charged with protecting these, day and night. In some districts, Gujranwala for example, the martial law administrator, Colonel O'Brian, ordered Indians to alight from their carriages and salute British Officers if they happened to pass them in the street. One of the things most hated about these laws was the increased police power. The laws were all enforced by the police.

A rigorous censorship of the press was imposed, keeping news of the Punjab restricted. Mahatma Gandhi was prohibited from entering the region. The barrister Eardley Norton, an Englishman who had offered legal aid to all Indians; C.F Andrews, Gandhi's friend from his days in South Africa; and B.G. Horniman of the *Bombay Chronicle* were all deported.

A wave of anger and sorrow ran throughout the country when news of the atrocities perpetrated in the Punjab came to be known. The government was forced by the adverse public opinion to appoint a commission of inquiry. General Dyer was reprimanded for his actions and asked to resign from the army, but he was permitted to retain his full pension benefits and other rights due him. His admirers in England collected a sum of twenty-six thousand pounds as a purse for him. The commission of inquiry had been nothing more than an eyewash to allay public opinion. The truth of the atrocities came out in a separate commission of inquiry appointed by the Indian National Congress.

It was in this atmosphere that our convent authorities decided to invite the Governor of the Punjab, Sir Michael O'Dwyer, a Catholic and patron of our school, to a special function in his honor. A purse was to be presented to him by the convent authorities and each student was asked to contribute four *annas*. It was made clear to us all that the contribution was by no means compulsory. Mother promptly took advantage of this proviso and refused to contribute anything. No action was taken against us at that time, although the authorities must have felt that it was a breach of discipline and an insult to the governor of the province.

At the 1919 session of the Indian National Congress in Amritsar in December, presided over by Pandit Motilal Nehru, Mother singlehandedly organized and ran a stall in the Congress *nagar* [township]. She had been asked to do so by Swami Shraddhanand. The proceeds of the sales were to be donated to the victims of martial law. The members of *kumari sabha* contributed items such as handmade embroidered tablecloths and lamp shades. My eldest sister Chandra was not very well at the time and had to be left in Lahore, so Mother traveled every morning to Amritsar and returned to Lahore at night. During the day, my sister was left in the care of my maternal grandfather and the servants. Needless to say, Grandfather thoroughly disapproved of such goings-on.

I had an uncle, a government servant posted at Amritsar, with whom we were always welcome to stay whenever we felt like it. During the Congress session, however, he made it clear to Mother that it would be more diplomatic if we did not visit him, much less stay with him. So Janak, Shyama, and I stayed with our uncle Pandit Shyam Lal Nehru and his wife Uma Nehru (who became a member of Parliament after Independence) in an apartment Mother had arranged for them just inside the Hall Bazaar Gate. I remember that Uncle used to sit at the window overlooking the road and invite all his friends for a cup of tea or a *pan* as they passed by. For us children, living in such a popular place with processions and crowds milling around was the best part of the Congress.

My sisters and I were in the Congress choir, singing national songs for the opening and other sessions. We were coached by Srimati Saraladevi Chaudhurani, a remarkable woman from Bengal and wife of the veteran Congress leader of the Punjab, Rambhaj Dutt Chaudhri. In addition, Mother gave Krishna (Motilal Nehru's younger daughter), Shyama, and I trays of picture postcards, buttons, and other small items with instructions to roam around and sell these in the Congress *nagar* to supplement the income of Mother's stall. The three of us always stuck together, which caused some measure of exasperation and amusement for Jawaharlal, for as soon as he stepped out of the *pandal* [marquee], we would pester him to buy something from each tray. He often complained to Mother that payment made to one of us was never sufficient—all three of us had to have an equal share every time!

This was Mother's debut into public life. From then on she attended all public meetings. In those days very few women went out alone, but, because my father was in Allahabad, Mother went to meetings by herself. My maternal grandfather belonged to the old school, however. He could not get used to Mother going to these meetings at all, let alone unescorted. He would insist that she take a male servant with her. It so happened that in those days we had no adult servant, but only a young man who worked for us. Grandfather would insist that she take this fellow with her. Mother would protest that a young lad would not be much help should the need arise, to which Grandfather would reply that at least she would be accompanied by a male. The times were such that a grown-up married woman, living on her own with her children, still needed male protection.

My grandfather had lived all his life in Matti-Ka-Chowk in Shahalmi Gate, right in the heart of the city. He lived there all alone with only one servant and had all his friends around him. He certainly would not have welcomed a daughter to share his house, especially not one who flouted all the social norms and had four noisy female children. I remember Pandit Motilal once remarking that he thought only boys could make so much noise!

When Mrs. Sarojini Naidu* visited Lahore, Mother organized a women's reception for her. It was presided over by Rani Narendra Nath, Mother's aunt, and Lady Zulfiqur Ali Khan† and was the first joint Hindu–Muslim women's reception in Lahore. At another recep-

---

*Gandhi's faithful lieutenant and the most important woman leader at the time.
†Wife of an important Muslim politician.

tion, for Srimati Kamaladevi Chattopadhyay,* Mother persuaded Sir Mohammad Shafi† to preside over the function. When Gandhiji visited Lahore for his *harijan* [Gandhi's word for an untouchable, "Child of God"] tour in 1933, Mother collected donations from women and presented Srimati Kasturbai with a silver *lota* [vessel for keeping water]. Later, Mother collected a very large amount for the Behar earthquake sufferers. Thus, she was in the forefront of all public activity in Lahore.

Mahatma Gandhi launched the noncooperation movement on August 1, 1920. He advocated the use of cotton *khadi* [hand-spun, hand-woven cloth], which became the uniform of the Independence Movement. Everyone—man or woman, urbanite or peasant—was expected to spin yarn on the *charka* [spinning wheel], which became not only the symbol of a peaceful revolution, but also a means of *sadhana* [religious discipline] for purification of the people's lives and bringing them nearer to God. For Indians, appeals must have some element of spirituality to be successful. I remember our own *charka* in Lahore. It was beautiful, and colorful as well, painted in soft shades of blue and red, studded with glass bells that would tinkle as the wheel was turned. Even before Gandhiji had advocated *charka*, spinning used to be a favorite pastime of even affluent ladies in the Punjab. In this part of the country the *charka* was fashioned in different colors to make it a pleasure to work on. The yarn spun was used mostly for making thick and colorful bed covers, either for use by the family or for charitable donation.

As part of the movement, the public were asked to give up their offices, titles, courts, colleges, councils, and services. At the Congress session in December of that year, the attainment of *swaraj* by peaceful and legitimate means had become the country's aim. *Swadeshi* meant wearing hand-spun, hand-woven cloth and using only indigenous goods. The boycott was to cover all foreign goods. Even the visit of the Prince of Wales was boycotted in 1921. Gandhiji had planned a no-tax campaign in Bardoli Subdivision, Bombay Presidency, but this plan had to be given up because of an outbreak of violence at Chauri Chaura in Gorakhpur District, Uttar Pradesh. Twenty-one constables and one subinspector of police were burned alive in the police station

---

*One of the founders of the All-India Women's Congress.
†Important Muslim politician from the Punjab.

where they had taken shelter. This caused Gandhiji, who abhorred violence in any form, to call off the planned civil disobedience movement. Gandhiji said that the British wanted us to fight on their terms, but they had weapons and we did not. Therefore, he said, we had to put the struggle on terms where we did have weapons.

In March 1922 Gandhiji was arrested and sentenced to six years imprisonment. He was released on January 12, 1924, before the expiration of his term. This earlier noncooperation movement was confined largely to men and was less extensive than the *satyagraha* movement of 1930–32. Women were expected to participate in processions and attend all Congress meetings, however, so with Mother and my two older sisters, Chandra and Janak, I used to join all such functions. I would like my readers to visualize the restricted life women led, even in a province so progressive as the Punjab. Women hardly ever ventured beyond the four walls of their homes, except to visit relatives or to attend a religious festival. My mother's aunt always wore a shawl over her sari when she went visiting. I suppose that could be considered as a sort of Hindu *burqa* [cloak worn by secluded women] although her face was left uncovered. In that atmosphere, for the women to leave their homes and walk in a procession was a big step forward. The present footwear, *chappals* [sandals], had just come into fashion, and women unused to walking any distance in a disciplined manner found it extremely difficult to walk in their *chappals*. The *chappals* would come off as the women walked in procession. They could not pause to put them on again and usually continued walking barefoot in the procession. Mother had two Congress volunteers walk behind the women. Their duty was to pick up any odd *chappal* left behind, put it in a cloth bag, and bring it back to the office of the District Congress Committee at Pari Mahal, where the procession usually terminated. The women would reclaim their footwear and then go home. This was the training period. Later, these women would come into their own and storm the citadels of the mighty British Empire.

The main work of the women, as envisaged by the Congress, was to propagate the use of *khadi*. Women appealed to other women to discard foreign cloth. A number of songs were composed to bring this point home. Not all families could afford to throw away their clothes and buy a completely new wardrobe, but all the women had a couple of *khadi* saris, which they wore to all the meetings and processions. It was extremely difficult to forego buying the lovely materials available;

in contrast, *khadi* was coarse and rough and not easily available. Our own textile industry had been completely destroyed by the British. It is said that the Indian muslin was so fine and soft that an entire sari could pass through a ring. All the foreign cloth collected by Congress would be consigned to the flames in a huge bonfire, held on the banks of the river Ravi. I remember one occasion vividly. It was wintertime and the river had receded, leaving a small sandy island in the middle. The bonfire was set there, where it looked dramatic and was good for publicity.

Another incident is very clearly etched in my mind. A public meeting was to be held at Bradlaugh Hall, and Mother, Chandra, Janak, and I were going there in a *tonga*. We did not know that the hall had been occupied by the police and that the venue of the meeting had been moved to another place in the heart of the city. En route to the meeting, we were accosted by a stranger who informed us in a whisper that the meeting was being held at such and such a place. Instead of proceeding to Bradlaugh Hall, Mother directed the *tonga* driver to take us to this other place. On the way, she kept wondering whether our informant was a reliable friend or a secret service man trying to prevent us from attending the meeting. When we arrived at our destination, we found that our informant had been correct and the meeting was in progress. I have forgotten the name of that place, but it was a sort of miniature Jallianwala *Bagh*, surrounded by tall houses and having only one entry. As the meeting progressed, the police walked in armed with metal-tipped *lathis* [sticks]. They declared the meeting illegal and requested that all women leave. The women understood that the men would be beaten once they left, so they refused to go. The excitement was intense and I was shouting slogans at the top of my voice. Those were the days when the British still remembered their chivalry. The police were not authorized to *lathi*-charge the men for fear of hitting the women. They tried persuasion and finally permitted the organizers to wind up the meeting and disperse. What a triumphant procession we made, parading through the streets of Lahore, celebrating our victory through nonviolence. Slogans were raised all along the route. I was only eleven years old and my excitement knew no bounds.

When I was twelve or thirteen, and Shyama, poor girl, was even younger, we were put in *khadi* saris. We never had ribbons or lace after that. Andhra Pradesh had started producing very fine *khadi*, but it was not enough for the whole country. We were a large family, four girls and Mother, all wearing saris, and it was impossible to get so much *khadi*. The order had to be placed months in advance, as it took a long time to complete. But we were so proud of our dress that we refused to wear anything else. In 1922, when my two cousins got married at Amritsar, Mother had ordinary white *khadi* dyed in different colors and printed in gold or silver so that we would look as dressy as our other girl cousins for such a grand occasion. We never complained that Mother had given all her lovely silk saris to be burned in the bonfires.

Kashmiri women are very simple in their dress. Summer or winter, they usually wear cotton at home. In Allahabad, before Gandhiji started his noncooperation movement, Mother used to wear cotton in summer and her old silk saris in winter. She came in for a lot of criticism by other women in the family for being so fashionable.

About this time, I fell ill with a bad attack of typhoid fever. In all, I had three relapses and was very seriously ill for about four months. Dr. Beli Ram was a very well known physician in Lahore and a good friend of my grandfather. So when I fell ill, the latter went to call on him. We were living in Bharat Buildings on the first floor in those days, and although he lived in a narrow lane in the city, Dr. Beli Ram asked my grandfather to bring the patient to his clinic there. On being informed that I was in no condition to be moved, Dr. Beli Ram agreed to come to me, but positively refused to climb the stairs to our flat. As a special concession to his friendship with Grandfather, he agreed to climb halfway up to the flat and insisted that I be carried on a chair halfway down to the landing so that he could examine me. Mother vetoed this preposterous suggestion. She then sent for Dr. Hira Lal. No one realized that he was a surgeon and not a physician, nor did he straighten out this misunderstanding when he came to see me. He prescribed a dose of castor oil and went home. Mother and the nurse in attendance protested that castor oil was fatal to a typhoid patient, but the doctor's orders had to be obeyed. I was dosed with castor oil, and my temperature soared. Gone were all hopes for my recovery. I think Dr. Hira Lal must have consulted some books after he went home and realized his grave mistake. Early the next morning, when my grandfather went to call on him (he lived quite near) he said he was just coming. He never came, and, after waiting for a couple of hours, Mother sent my cousin Sham Sunder to call on him again, impressing on him the critical condition of his patient. Sham Sunder was told that the doctor had left his house for some unknown destination. Mother was naturally very upset. She heard by chance that Dr. Bal Kishan Kaul, a well-known physician, was in Lahore for a few days. Dr. Kaul usually went to Kashmir for the summer months, so we had been bereft of his advice. Mother went to see him immediately and relayed everything. He told her to call Dr. Udho Ram and assured her that he would come himself. He left instructions with Dr. Udho Ram, who took full charge of the case. I think he got a lot of publicity for this, because wherever he went he was asked about the case "ruined" by Dr. Hira Lal. My father was preparing a legal suit against Dr. Hira Lal when we heard that a young son of Dr. Hira Lal's had also fallen ill with typhoid fever and died. Father decided to give up the idea of filing a lawsuit against him.

As I mentioned, we were living on the first floor in Bharat Buildings. The ground floor was occupied by a group of students, brothers and sisters who were studying in various colleges in Lahore. One of the girls, Sushila Bali, was studying with my eldest sister, Chandra, at Kinnaird College. At the end of the term, these young men and women went home. The father of these students, Dina Nath Bali, had photography shops in Rawalpindi and Murree, with houses in both places. When he heard about my illness, he was very upset and reprimanded his sons for leaving Lahore when they could have been of some help to Mother. Anyway, his wife wrote to Mother offering a couple of rooms in their house in Murree to stay for as long as we wanted once I had recovered enough to travel. That was exactly what we did. As the Bali family were very strict vegetarians, their only condition was that Mother cook neither meat nor eggs while we were in their house.

It so happened that my doctor, Udho Ram, was also a strict vegetarian. He resisted all Mother's attempts to feed me meat broth. He kept me on a strict vegetarian diet. Surprisingly enough, although we lived in Lahore for many years after 1920 (when I had this bout of fever), we never met Dr. Udho Ram again.

I had to stay at home for six months, recuperating, and all in all I was away from school for almost a year. My class had been promoted from standard 4 to 5 and had already begun to study algebra and geometry. Actually, Mother would not have permitted me to attend school when I did, but she had to go away from Lahore for some Congress work and could not leave me alone in the house. She therefore asked the convent authorities if I could sit in class without doing any lessons. I did so, but all my longing to be with my friends and my loneliness at home were poignantly brought home to me. When Mother returned, I wept and pleaded until I was allowed to attend school as a regular student again. Sister Juliet, my class teacher, agreed to take me in standard 5, provided I made up the lost ground at home. With the help of my sister Chandra, I tried to, but it was never the same. My grounding in these two subjects, algebra and geometry, remained weak, and my grades dropped. Then Vijayalakshmi's wedding intervened, and my sister, also my tutor, could spare very little time for me during the wedding festivities. Actually, I should never have been permitted to join a higher class when I had missed so much due to my illness.

Vijayalakshmi Pandit, Motilal Nehru's eldest daughter, was married in May 1921. All the top Congress leaders had come to *Anand Bhavan* to attend the wedding. The groom, Ranjit S. Pandit, was a man from outside the Kashmiri community, a Brahmin from Saurashtra. The bride wore a *khadi* sari, the yarn of which had been specially spun for her by Gandhiji. The wedding was very simple and austere. Mother had new frocks made for my younger sister Shyama and myself and new saris for my two older sisters. When we got to Allahabad we found the entire family, both men and women, wearing coarse *khadi* and feeling very proud of themselves. Mother asked Father to procure *khadi* saris for all of us immediately. *Khadi* was still not easily available. Gandhiji's village industries program had not taken deep roots. Father had to send both his *munshis* to nearby villages to buy whatever was available. I will never forget those dark, multicolored saris we wore so proudly.

Weddings were important occasions for our family. My memories of them are vivid. In May 1927, my eldest sister, Chandra, married a young Kashmiri man, Sri Krishna Handoo, in Allahabad. His family had lived in Madras for many years and had migrated to Allahabad when all their daughters were married. One of Sri Krishna's sisters, Dhanwanti (later Lady Rama Rao), was the first Kashmiri girl to pass her master's examination. Because she was so highly qualified, no young man from our community was prepared to marry her. This did not worry her parents, who were very broad-minded. They married her to a young south Indian ICS (Indian Civil Service) officer, Benegal Rama Rao, who rose to high office under the British Government and was later knighted. We had met the Handoo family when we went to

Allahabad for our vacation. I believe that Sri Krishna was interested in my sister Chandra, who was the second in the community to earn her master's, and persuaded his mother to invite us over. Sri Krishna joined the Imperial Bank (as the State Bank was then known) and finally retired as managing director of that institution.

When the date of their wedding was fixed, Shyama and I were both in the hostel in Kinnaird College. I was in my third year there, while Shyama had just joined. Mother had temporarily closed up the house in Lahore to make arrangements for the wedding. Generally, weddings are very elaborate affairs. My sister Janak was living in the YWCA hostel, appearing for her master's final in English. She would go to Allahabad once her examinations were over, but both Shyama and I were very keen to be there a few days ahead of the festivities. The problem was how to get to Allahabad. We had never traveled alone and knew that Father would not approve of it. So Mother wrote to her aunt, Rani Narendra Nath, to ask if she could arrange to send her old retainer Khera with us as an escort. Unfortunately, Khera was on leave. Rani Narendra Nath could think of no other employee of hers who would be as reliable, so there we were, all set to go to Allahabad, but there was no escort. Mother finally wrote to say that she had Father's permission for both of us to travel unescorted to Delhi, where she would meet us. On arrival there we would be met by our uncle, Braj Lal Nehru, spend the day with him, meet Mother, and travel to Allahabad the same night. I have never been able to understand why Father would not permit us to go straight to Allahabad. Having reached Delhi, we could have boarded the Kalka-Delhi-Howrah Mail and continued our journey by day, reaching Allahabad the same night. It would have saved Mother the extra journey.

With Father's permission, Shyama and I left for Delhi by Frontier Mail, traveling in a second-class compartment. The railway compartments in those days were quite different from what they are now. The windows were broad and wide, with no bars, and the padded leather seats were very comfortable. Traveling in those days was much safer and far more fun than it is now. A variety of small knickknacks were on sale at all the stations. Shyama and I were alone in the compartment and kept one light on the whole night. We were nervous because we had never traveled alone and took turns keeping watch.

At one of the stations, an Anglo-Indian guard noticed this. He understood immediately that we were too frightened and nervous to relax and sleep, so he assured us that he would stand in front of our compartment at all stations and see that no one entered. Then we slept comfortably. We reached Delhi, met Mother, who had come by night train as well, and continued to our destination.

We enjoyed the wedding with our cousins and friends in spite of the heat of Allahabad. It is customary in our community that on such ceremonial occasions, both men and women sit down together for meals either on a *pucca* [solid] floor, or on a low *takhtposh*, half of which is covered with a cotton carpet to sit on, while the other half is left uncovered for the food. Another accepted convention was that on such occasions the food was served on large plates called *pattals*. Water was served in earthenware glasses called *kulhar* [earthenware]. These were all washed, cleaned, and dried beforehand and thrown away after use.

Although we had large lawns both in front and back of our house, Mother had arranged for the *barat* and the guests to have dinner on the terrace of our house. I suppose that was to catch whatever little breeze there was on that hot day. Vijayalakshmi and her non-Kashmiri husband, Ranjit Pandit, were also present at the wedding. Another custom among us is that food is served by the family members, usually by the younger generation, with the elders supervising. Vijayalakshmi was among the servers, and Mother had persuaded Ranjit to sit and eat with the bridegroom's party. A very good friend of our family, Madan Mohan Raina, was also sitting with the guests. Mother noticed that he was not eating anything, but every time she asked him if the food was not to his liking, he would say, "No, no Lado Bhabi, I am just about to start"; but he would not eat. Mother was mystified until she realized that according to orthodox Kashmiri custom, no non-Kashmiri is permitted to join the community on such an occasion. But we had Ranjit sitting with the guests. Madan Raina must have felt that since it was a Kashmiri wedding all the traditional rules should be observed, but, out of respect for my parents, he could not refuse to join the *barat* for dinner. He was an advocate, and when he joined the Allahabad High Court, he became my father's junior and had lived in our house for a considerable time. So he sat with the diners but did not eat.

At another wedding in Lahore, the leaders of the Kashmiri community approached the bride's father, Arjan Nath Atal, and informed him that women like my mother, Kamla Nehru, Kamla's mother, Mrs. Rajpati Kaul, and one or two others were much too "forward." These leaders warned that if these women attended the wedding, the community in general would be compelled to boycott it. In those days, no invitation cards were sent; the entire community was expected to attend the wedding. A list of all the Kashmiri families in town was prepared by the pandit, and this list of the wedding was circulated. People were expected to attend all functions. Mr. Atal replied that all the women mentioned by the community leaders were close relations and could not be excluded, but he said those members of the community who felt strongly about the whole affair need not join in the celebrations. Every one of them attended!

When we lived in Lahore we used to go to the theater when the Alfred Theatrical Company from Calcutta was in town. The entire balcony would be reserved for us and our friends. The servants would go ahead, remove the chairs, and spread a carpet with cushions. Those of us who wanted to sleep while the play was in progress could do so. The ubiquitous *pan-dans* went with us. Although Shyama and I were very young and should have been in bed, we went because Mother could not leave us alone in the house. Although it was past midnight when the play was over, we enjoyed ourselves very much. All the actors were men, even those playing women's roles. I remember one play that focused on King Bhagirath persuading Mother Ganges to come down to Earth. When this particular scene was enacted, religious fervor was so intense that the audience showered the stage with coins and notes as offerings to Mother Ganges. The theatrical company must have collected a large sum in addition to the proceeds from ticket sales!

Among our friends were members of a Kashmiri family who lived in the old traditional manner. The men occupied the outer portion of the house, while women and children occupied the inner courtyard. The head of the family, Pandit Shiv Narayan Raina, was an awe-inspiring figure. He kept very much to himself. When the ladies of this family visited the theater, they did so secretly. One night the electricity went off and the old gentleman came to the women's quarters. When the lights came on, he found that his daughter and his younger daughter-in-law were not at home. When he asked where they were, his eldest daughter-in-law got confused and said they had gone to visit my mother. He asked why they were visiting Lado Rani so late at night and was told that they had gone to pay their respects to Gandhiji, who was dining with Mother. Fortunately, Gandhiji was visiting Lahore in those days, so the ruse worked. No one recalled that Gandhiji was very abstemious in his habits and had only goat's milk and a little fruit early in the evening, certainly not an elaborate Indian dinner.

Many years later we spent a few days with the old gentleman, whom we all addressed as "Papaji." We found him charming and lovable, and full of old world courtesy, but very lonely. We wondered why we had been so much in awe of him. In our youth, there had been no social interaction between the young men of the family and us, although we were constantly in and out of their house. When Pandit Shiv Narayan's grandson, Chand Narayan, was going to England for further studies, he and his cousin Raja Atal came to say good-bye to Mother. We were still living in Bharat Buildings, so it must have been 1923 or early 1924, as we left that place for Panj Mahal Road sometime in 1924 due to an epidemic of plague in the city. When these two young men came, Mother was out and our cousin Krishna was staying with us. The question now arose, Who would entertain these men until Mother returned? The three of us and Krishna persuaded Chandra to entertain them. But such were the conventions of society in those days that Chandra would not sit alone with them in the drawing room, nor were the rest of us prepared to go and sit there with her to give her moral support. Finally poor Chandra was almost pushed by us into the drawing room. Chand Narayan and Raja Atal were equally embarrassed. Fortunately, Mother returned home and the tension was relieved.

Chandra passed her bachelor's degree in 1923. That year, we were spending our vacation with Pandit Motilal and his family on a small estate called Ghora Khal, a very small hill station belonging to the Nawab of Rampur. There were only two houses on the estate. The main one, built by the owner for himself, was occupied by Hakim Ajmal Khan, the royal physician of the Rampur family. The other, which was vacant at that time, was a very small cottage built by the Nawab for the engineer in charge of developing the estate. Hakim Ajmal Khan and Pandit Motilal looked upon each other as brothers. In India such a relationship is known as *dharam-ka-bhai*, meaning that religion looks upon them as brothers. Usually two friends of the same religion become *dharam-ka-bhai* by exchanging turbans. I do not think Pandit Motilal and Hakim Ajmal Khan had exchanged turbans, but their affection for each other was like that of real brothers. Hakim Ajmal Khan persuaded Pandit Motilal to occupy the vacant cottage.

In fact, I remember we were all set to go to Kashmir for our holidays that year. Father had come from Allahabad and all arrangements were complete when a telegram arrived from Pandit Motilal inviting us to Ghora Khal. Such was the respect and affection my parents had for him that no one dared say we were planning to go elsewhere. So we packed and left for Ghora Khal. It was really a very quiet place. All supplies—eggs, meat, vegetables, and so forth—came from Naini Tal, at a distance of seven miles through hilly roads. Ghora Khal was a treeless, rather hot place, so in the daytime we had to stay indoors. We got so fed up that we persuaded Pandit Motilal to take the whole family to Naini Tal. There we could go out riding or for long walks along the lake, so we liked Naini Tal very much. The house Pandit Motilal took there was two or three miles below the mall. It was a split-level house with the drawing room, a couple of bedrooms, and an office on the ground floor. Upstairs was a large hall which was used as a dining room and an Indian-style sitting room with carpets and cushions where Mrs. Motilal entertained her women visitors. Pandit Motilal and Mrs. Vijayalakshmi Pandit and her husband occupied the bedrooms downstairs. The rest of the family, Mrs. Motilal, Mrs. Kamla Nehru, and our whole family were upstairs.

Once a group of women came to visit, and Mrs. Motilal sent my mother to entertain them until she was free. The usual questions followed: How many children did Mother have and what were they doing? Whenever people heard that she had four daughters and no son, they would express their sorrow and end with a prayer to the Almighty God to grant her a son. Fed up with such commiserations, Mother had begun to inform everyone that she had two daughters and two sons. On being asked what the latter did, she would say that they were studying abroad. But this time she could not carry it off with her usual aplomb. The women became suspicious. So when Mrs. Motilal came and Mother left to see to the refreshments, these ladies repeated their questions. In all innocence, Mrs. Nehru replied that Mother had four daughters and no son. Needless to say, the women were very upset. They started calling out to Mother to come out and face them, remarking that being a disciple of Gandhiji she should not hide the truth from them. Poor Mother; she did not know how to face them and so would not leave her room.

At about this time, a meeting of the *Swaraj* party had been called by Pandit Motilal in Naini Tal. The *Swaraj* party had been formed in 1920 by Pandit Motilal, C.R. Das, and Hakim Ajmal Khan because they believed the British Government had to be fought on all fronts, even from inside the legislatures. Gandhiji was not in favor of this move; he wanted Indians to boycott all institutions. My sister Chandra had just passed her bachelor's examination and, being the first girl in the family to do so, was made much of. For this *Swaraj* party meeting, Congress leaders in favor of council entry met in the drawing room of our house. During one of the after-dinner meetings, we were banished to the upper floor and admonished not to make any noise. Mother, Vijayalakshmi, Ranjit, and Kamla Nehru naturally attended all sessions. Kamla asked Chandra to attend because she was now old enough (she was nineteen years old) to take an interest in her country's affairs. The four of us (Krishna included) considered Chandra one of our age-group and resented that she was being considered an adult by the family. As a prank, we decided to celebrate her graduation that same evening, so we got ahold of all kinds of metal kitchen utensils to bang on and shouted from the banisters for Chandra to come upstairs. Kamla told her not to go because they could hear our suppressed giggles and knew something was wrong. Chandra was bored sitting in that august assembly and did not heed Kamla's advice. The moment she put her foot on the top-most step, we started beating the metal utensils and created so much noise that the meeting must have been disturbed. You can imagine how sporting Pandit Motilal was and the affection he had for us that he took it all as a joke and never once reprimanded us! Truly he was a great and wonderful man.

In most Indian families, the head of the family rarely eats with the rest of the members. In our family, there was so much goodwill that at mealtimes the whole family sat together. Pandit Motilal was a family man in the true sense of the word and liked to have all his children around him. Of course at that time we were usually on our best behavior.

I have precious memories of the times we spent with Pandit Motilal. Out of all his nephews and their families, I think we spent most of our holidays with him. I suppose this is one of the reasons why we were so close to him. Krishna used to come and spend months with us. She was a lonely child, there being so much difference in age between her and her brother and her elder sister. The moment news would come of

Pandit Motilal's planned visit to Lahore, I would pester him with letters pleading that he bring Krishna with him and permit her to stay with us for an indefinite period. The family had already plunged into the freedom struggle. The English governess had married and retired. Pandit Motilal was not in favor of sending Krishna to school, so she was happiest staying with us. We were a large family of four, all girls, and there was always something going on at home. Life was very restricted in that we were not permitted to go to the cinema or to restaurants, but we managed to amuse ourselves and never had a dull moment. No one dreamed of having a bedroom to herself. Instead, we lived more as a community, where we learned the principles of give and take.

After the noncooperation movement of 1920, the police started raiding *Anand Bhavan* in Allahabad, taking away valuable carpets and other items in lieu of the fines imposed on Motilal and Jawaharlal. All bank accounts, securities, and so forth, were transferred to my father's name so that Mrs. Motilal and the immediate family would not suffer any hardship. Life changed drastically. Carriages and horses were dispensed with. There was no lavish entertainment, nor were there two kitchens. Life had become simple for those left behind, and it centered around the activities of the local Congress committee and prison visits. My father took his responsibilities very seriously and used to visit his aunt, Mrs. Motilal, every day to see to her comfort. After Krishna got married in October 1933, I used to visit Mrs. Motilal every evening to sit and chat with her and try to cheer her up. It was the least we could do for her after all that she and Pandit Motilal had done for us.

The years after the suspension of the noncooperation movement were uneventful. Gandhiji, who could gauge the pulse of the nation, felt that people were not ready for the major thrust of the nonviolent struggle, so he bided his time and launched the constructive side of his program by asking people to take up spinning and weaving in earnest. Rural folks were especially enjoined to do so between sowing and harvesting their crops. To assist them, Gandhi founded the All-India Village and Khadi Industries Organization. He also propagated the removal of "untouchability" by forming a *Harijan* Welfare Board. Under his inspiring leadership, educationists, like our late President Dr. Zakir Hussain, founded the *Jamia Milia Islamia* and "basic education" based on a totally new concept of education.

3

My Education

In 1922 we were still enrolled in the Sacred Heart Convent School in Lahore. That year, Roman Catholic dignitaries from Belgium were scheduled to visit. We were being coached to sing the Belgian national anthem. Since the imposition of martial law in 1919, "*Vande Mataram*" [Hail to the Motherland] had come to be regarded as India's national anthem. Written by the famous Bengali novelist Bankim Chandra Chatterjee, the text appeared first in his novel, *Ananda Math* [Monastery of Happiness]. It was set to music by the poet Rabindra Nath Tagore. Mother insisted that if the Belgium National Anthem was to be sung, "*Vande Mataram*" should also be included. The sisters of the convent regarded this as a harmless Indian song and readily agreed.

At one of the rehearsals an Indian asked the Mother Superior if she knew the meaning of this song. She did not. When she was told what it meant, the decision was made to withdraw it from the program. Mother was so incensed that she withdrew my younger sister Shyama and myself from the school in protest. In vain Sister Mary sent verbal requests through me for Mother to go and see her. An uncle and aunt had arrived from Srinagar for a visit, and since Mother was busy in the kitchen, she would not budge. We were living close enough to the convent to walk to school. I do not remember how many times I walked home from school and back again carrying messages. Neither Sister Mary nor Mother was prepared to put anything in writing. I think Sister Mary wanted us to stay in school, and if Mother had found time to go to talk it over, everything could have been settled amicably. Mother was anxious to secure a good education for her daughters, but she was not prepared to sacrifice her loyalty to her country. Although "*Vande Mataram*" had been accepted by the convent authorities without understanding its meaning, it was our national anthem and Mother could not tolerate any insult when the country's honor was at stake. It was not only Shyama and I who suffered by leaving school; both my older sisters, Chandra and Janak, were in the college section of the convent, and they also had to leave. In fact, Sister Mary had explained to the college girls why the Indian song had to be withdrawn. It was my elder sisters who came home and informed Mother. Shyama and I were shocked to hear that we were to leave school immediately. Mother was not prepared to wait for the end of the term or even for the next morning. Her country's honor came first, and she refused to compromise even when the education of her daughters was at stake. Fortunately, Janak was able to join Kinnaird College for Women, a very popular missionary institution. Chandra, under Gandhiji's influence, wanted to join a National College. There were some suggestions that Congress would start a college, but nothing came of it. So, after sitting at home for a few months waiting for Congress's college to materialize, Chandra also joined Kinnaird College, from which she graduated.

I joined the Lady Maclagan School for Girls and was admitted to the ninth class, that is, prematriculation. But when Lahore College for Women, a government institution, was opened, the ninth and tenth classes were transferred there from the Lady Maclagan School. At that time, Lahore College offered only the intermediate examination of the University of the Punjab. The degree classes were added much later. The educational system was very different then. Joining a college meant four years of study; that is, two years for the intermediate degree of the faculty of arts, as it was known, then two years of degree classes or bachelor of arts classes.

I started attending classes at Lahore College but was not allowed to appear for the matriculation examination because I was only fourteen years of age (the age limit was fifteen years). Consequently, I had to spend two years in the tenth class. While one class was sitting for their final examination and the old ninth class was not yet promoted to the tenth class, there was a gap of three or four months when no one knew what to do with me. My own class was appearing for their examination, and the new tenth class had not arrived yet, so one of my teachers, Mrs. Hem Raj, suggested to Mother that I take up domestic science as a sort of stopgap arrangement. Domestic science had just been offered as a subject, and the new teacher, Miss Graham, had arrived from England but had not properly settled down in her new home. She thought it was a good idea to have her house cleaned up. I was asked to clean and polish her windows as a part of the domestic science course. I got so disgusted that I told Mother I would rather sit at home and wait for the new term.

Poor Shyama had to sit at home for two years. In the Sacred Heart Convent the curriculum was all in English. Shyama was only eleven years of age when she was sent to the Lady Maclagan School with me. She had to join the middle school section, where all subjects were taught in the vernacular—either Hindi or Urdu. Shyama was unable to follow what was being taught so Mother withdrew her from school. She had to take lessons from my eldest sister, Chandra, until she was thirteen years of age, when she joined the Lahore College for Women in the ninth class. In most schools, other than the convent schools, subjects were taught in the vernacular until the ninth class when all subjects were suddenly switched to English. I had come from the Sacred Heart Convent and my English was good so I was immediately admitted to the ninth class in Lady Maclagan School. But English was considered Shyama's weakness. In the convent, Hindi was taught by the nuns themselves, and their knowledge of that language was not very good. They pronounced some words incorrectly, so Shyama was not well versed in Hindi either. I always wondered why no pandit or *maulvi* [Muslim scholar] was engaged to teach these two Indian languages.

In 1924 I too joined Kinnaird College, which had been set up to provide higher education for girls graduating from Kinnaird School. Both were missionary institutions and meant primarily for Indian Christian girls, but in the early 1920s, the principal of the college, Miss Edwards, was keen to admit non-Christian girls. That is why both of my elder sisters and one of my cousins, Kamla Dar, were studying there. At that time the college was housed in three bungalows with a large compound near the Lahore Railway Station. It had no proper boundary wall except one made of trellis work. The premises were rented and the college authorities were looking for suitable permanent accommodations. One bungalow housed the staff, one was used as a student hostel, and the third included an office, a library, a visitors'/ dining room, and a couple of classrooms. We had our classes in tents. Vernacular classes, that is, classes taught in Hindi, Urdu, and Sanskrit, were held under shady trees. Since there was no wall, any marriage procession passing by with a band was a great attraction. We used to plead with our teacher, Panditji, until we got permission to run to the trellis fence and watch the marriage procession go by.

Much against my parents' wishes I had taken up Sanskrit as my compulsory Indian language and Hindi as my optional language. I suffered from severe migraine headaches in those days, and the attacks, which came three or four times a month, would send me to bed for four days at a time. That is why my parents were against my taking up a subject which would require a lot of hard work. But I was then keen on getting my master's degree in Sanskrit. My other subjects were history, philosophy, and English. For some reason, subjects like economics were not offered to women students, although we could take up mathematics. Subjects like geography, botany, and zoology were unheard of, and of course there were no science courses. The college did not have scientific equipment, so the choice of subjects was very limited.

Those of us in Kinnaird College enjoyed a lot of freedom considering the times. The staff believed in democratic methods and encouraged student participation in the running of the college. We had a student council headed by a senior student (generally from the fourth year) who was elected by the entire student body. She was in charge of the general administration, that is, cleanliness and tidiness, of the hostel. She made the rounds of the rooms to see that the beds were properly made and clothes and books put away. Then there was the roll call, after morning prayers, attended by the entire female staff and all the students. The senior student was a buffer between the staff and students. No student was ever reprimanded directly by a staff member. Instead, the senior student was called to the office, the offense was explained, and she was requested to have a word with the culprit. It worked very well. It was the senior student who gave permission for walks or shopping trips. The rules were set and all the students had to do was to follow them. For example, first-year students could not go out together without a chaperone and, of course, a fourth-year student could go out alone. A warden had the overall charge of the hostel. The senior student had to report to her and get the leave register countersigned. All home leave was sanctioned by the warden herself.

At mealtimes the senior student was required to say grace. Kinnaird was a missionary college, so attendance at morning and evening prayers (the latter for hostelers only) was compulsory. The staff member who conducted the evening prayers had her dinner with the girls. Bible classes were also compulsory, and, since they were held immediately after the lunch break, you can imagine how trying they were. The girls were sleepy and took little or no interest in this class. The non-Christian girls were especially uncooperative. They adopted a passive attitude, and nothing that the professor said made any difference to them. The staff tried to make these classes as interesting as they could by talking about the message of the *Gita* or Mahatma Gandhi's philosophy, but it did not help. We had the same attitude toward prayers. But the hymns were so beautiful that one often felt the urge to join in the singing. One of my cousins (a day student) took a hymnbook home so that she could sing at her leisure.

In 1926, the college moved to Lake Road, opposite the university playing fields. Although there were still only three bungalows, the compound was huge and everything was better arranged, with room for classes in each house. We had a tennis court as well as badminton and basketball courts, so the girls could play more organized games. Women's higher education was still in its infancy, so the total number of girls was barely fifty. This kept the atmosphere friendly.

As this was a Christian college originally meant for Christian girls, no non-Christian girl had ever been elected to the office of senior student until I was elected in my fourth year. I was elected to this august post by a small margin, much to the chagrin of the Christian students. I agreed to say grace at mealtimes but put my foot down to the saying of "amen." That was left to the Christian girls. Thinking back now, it was rather silly of me to stick to such foolish ideas. There was no harm in saying "amen" after grace, and the mere saying of it would not have made me a Christian, but such are the foibles of youth. Generally, I got on extremely well with members of my class, most of whom were Christians. My best friend was an Indian Christian girl, Kamola Banerjea, and, with my parents' permission, I went to spend a few days with her family. I attended all the Christmas sales organized by the National Missionary Society and helped out at the stalls. Occasionally my younger sister Shyama and I would also accompany the Christian girls to church.

I was very keen on public speaking in those days and took an active part in all college debates; usually I preferred speaking from the floor rather than being one of the speakers for or against the motion. However, I once represented my college in an intercollegiate debate held at the Government College for Men.

While I was in my fourth year, two foreign women visited our college and spoke in glowing terms about the Tata School for Social Sciences just started in Bombay. Interested in social work, I was greatly impressed by what I had heard and promptly asked Father's permission to join this institution after my graduation. My poor, dear father, living in a quiet place like Allahabad, had never heard of such an institution and would not permit any of his daughters to deviate from the course already accepted by him. Both my older sisters had their master's degrees, one in philosophy and the other in English, and that was the highest degree to which he would agree. I had only two options: either join the master's class after graduation or sit at home. No fancy courses for him. Had I been permitted to join the Tata School for Social Sciences, I would have been one of the very few trained social workers in this part of the country.

During the summer vacation, whenever we were in Allahabad, our favorite pastime was spending the day at our Uncle Shamlal Nehru's house playing cards or gossiping with our cousins and friends. Sometimes a picnic would be arranged, and we used to go boating on the Ganges, visiting places like Jhusi, or we would go across the Phaphamau Bridge to the house of a *rana* [prince] exiled from Nepal. The *rana*'s son Parakram Jang was my age and a very good friend, as was Dr. Kalash Nath Katju's son Shiv Nath (Shivji). But most of our summer vacations were spent in the hills. While in Srinagar, Mother would hire a *donga* [small houseboat] and remove all the furniture to have more room. One of my cousins, Kala, was married and living in Srinagar, and she and her little son Narendra (Nanna) sometimes came to stay with us. We used to glide up the Jhelum River to Ganderbal on one side or to Anantnag on the other side, taking days for the journey. It was great fun, and, whenever we felt like it, we would get off the boat and walk along the banks or wander off in the fields and then join the *donga* at some point. It was not difficult, as the *donga*, like the kitchen boat and the *shikara* [small boat], was towed by three or four men, so of course it moved slowly. We used to get our vegetables, milk, and eggs from the villages we passed. Once we spent several days in Ganderbal, where we were joined by some friends from Lahore who had also hired a houseboat. Ganderbal was a very quiet and picturesque place with lovely trees and little streams meandering along until they joined the river. If we got tired of walking there was always the *shikara*, which formed a sort of free transport as it went along with the *donga*. My cousin Kala had married into a Kashmiri joint family, very old and wealthy residents of Srinagar, who lived on the Third Bridge or Habba Kadal, as it was called. Her husband had a number of young male cousins who always came along with him to our boat. With those young men as our escorts, we would indulge in all kinds of mad pranks. Late at night, we tried to climb straight up to the Shankaracharya temple. There was a full moon that night, but there was not even a foot path and we lost our way. How we shouted to Triloki Bhai (Kala's husband), who had given up the climb at an early stage and was sitting almost at the base, to give us some indications where we were so that we could come down safely. Our attempt to find a shortcut from Dal Lake to the temple failed miserably.

The time we spent at Achabal is very memorable. The maharaja had an old and beautiful Mughal garden open to the public during the day. It had lovely lawns with shallow, canal-like streams running on both sides of the lawns shaded with large chinar trees. Since there was no hotel and not even a *dharamshala* [pilgrim shelter], visitors had to camp in tents in the open spaces just outside the garden. On one of our visits, an uncle who lived in Srinagar made arrangements for tents and sent his wife and teenage son with us. It so happened that there was a spate of burglaries at that time, and Mother felt very insecure with only one young male (my cousin) in our party. The maharaja's guru was staying in one of the *baradaree* [open shelter with roof] inside the garden, and Mother asked if we could stay inside the garden in one of the old buildings. He graciously consented, and we stayed in a two-story building with solid floors but no toilet facilities. We arranged to cook on the first floor, and, for our baths, Mother had a *choldari* [a very small tent] pitched across one of the streams that ran in the garden. We sat on a wooden plank placed across the stream for our morning ablutions. Getting hot water was out of the question so we bathed in that cold running water.

We spent our days under the chinar trees. All four of us had engraved our initials on them, and if they are still standing one could probably see them still. One foreign woman, an artist, was sharing the shelter of those trees and offered us some fruit. Thinking that as Hindus we might object, she assured us that it was not peeled and therefore remained "untouched" by her. We promptly accepted the offer and assured her that we did not belong to such an old-fashioned family.

As Mother did not like to stay in one place for vacation, we were able to visit other hill stations in the Punjab. On one of our visits to Dalhousie, we had a house called Dilkusha on the lower part of Bakrota Hill. After evening walks along the mall, most of the residents living along lower Bakrota would return by the same road. On one occasion we noticed that Mother and the four of us were being followed by half a dozen British soldiers. They were obviously from the cantonment called Bakloh and stopped in the road before we turned in our gate. After dinner I decided to stroll out to the open space in front of the house and look down onto the road. Imagine my surprise when I saw the glow of three or four cigarettes in the darkness. I went inside and told Mother that I thought the soldiers were still standing below. She immediately sent word to some friends living just above us for help, and the young men from there came rushing out armed with *lathis* and chased the soldiers away. The next morning, Mother complained by letter to the commanding officer of the cantonment. What action, if any, was taken we do not know, but the soldiers were never seen on the mall in Dalhousie again.

Another time we went there rather late in the year; summer was almost over. Raja Narendra Nath, my mother's uncle, had rented a large house for the season, but for some reason or another could not go himself, so he offered the house to Mother for the remainder of the season. Normally we resented taking special leave from school or college, but that year we agreed. We went to Dalhousie, taking our two cousins Kamla and Khem with us. Father and Krishna joined us from Allahabad. During our sojourn there, it rained and hailed. We enjoyed that hailstorm more than anything else. We carried every receptacle we could find out into the open to catch the hailstones. Although it became very cold, we had the time of our lives. My cousin Kamla was a very effective storyteller. Tired of collecting hailstones, Krishna, Shyama, and I persuaded Kamla to tell us a story. There we sat, huddled on a bed with quilts and blankets to keep us warm, and listened to Kamla tell us her version of *The Three Musketeers* by Alexandre Dumas. Of course the story was not completed in one sitting, but we were housebound for several days waiting for the hailstones to melt. What more enjoyable pastime could the three of us have had!

There were no air services to any hill station in those days. Often we had to travel the hard way, but we saw more of the countryside and enjoyed it more. Sometimes I feel sorry for today's younger generation. With air services and deluxe buses and trains, life has become more comfortable but not half as interesting or enjoyable.

Once Janak, Shyama, and I decided to learn how to horseback ride. It was easy to get Mother's permission, because she was keen that we learn as many things as we could. There used to be a cavalry remount depot somewhere in the civil lines, the area where British nonmilitary government personnel lived. Where it was exactly, I have no recollection, but I do know that it could not have been in the cantonments, as with our Congress background we would never have been permitted by the authorities to go anywhere near it. When we approached the officer in charge, he promptly agreed to let us learn to ride. We had jodhpurs made for ourselves and went every day to this remount depot. The horses were cavalry horses, so we were permitted to ride only in the enclosures reserved for exercising them. After some months we felt we had learned enough to go out on the public roads, but the instructor would not allow us to. He could not take the responsibility of looking after three girls at the same time, nor was he prepared to take us out one at a time. We were very keen to do this because we wanted to see how much we had really learned. You cannot really ride in a small enclosure, and we wanted to show off to our friends. No matter how much we pleaded, the instructor would not budge.

Looking back, I wonder whether he was permitted even to hire out the cavalry horses like this. He was a British army officer, and maybe he thought he could make extra money teaching three Indian girls to ride, but he could not risk disclosure by escorting us on public roads. So, reluctantly, we gave up our riding lessons as we could make no progress just going around and around that enclosure.

Years later, my husband-to-be, then in government service and posted in New Delhi, used to plan how we would join the riding club and go for early morning rides. But all that came to nothing, as he was not an early riser. Whatever riding I had learned in Lahore could never be practiced properly.

Shyama and I used to play tennis at the Cosmopolitan Club, but that was disrupted by our going in and out of prison for three years. Janak, Shyama, and I also learned *Kathak* dancing with a master in Lahore, but we could not continue our lessons once we matured.

All four of us were very fond of music, especially singing, and would indulge in a lot of casual singing. Any one of us, sitting in any corner of the house, had only to sing one bar of a particular song, and the refrain would be taken up by the rest of us, joining in from wherever we were, regardless of what we were doing. Even in the midst of serious studies we would stop for a time and join in the song. Mind you, no one ever moved so that all four of us could sit together and sing properly. Nor did we feel it necessary to finish the song. We never got together at a particular time just to indulge in our desire to sing. We all understood that our song was meant only as a form of temporary relaxation. Whoever was studying never raised any objection about being disturbed or losing a train of thought. The song would fade away just as it had begun, as one by one we dropped out. I do not remember where or how we picked up this habit. Mother was greatly amused by it, and later in life she would proudly recount to all her friends this peculiar habit of her daughters. I suppose the times we were living in, with an abundance of songs sung in processions and at meetings, made us feel very free about expressing ourselves this way.

4

The Lahore Congress, 1929

It was the year 1928. I had just been admitted as a postgraduate student at Government College for Men in Lahore (now in Pakistan). As my two older sisters had also completed their master's degrees at this institution, there was no difficulty over my admission. After my eldest sister's wedding, Mother decided to stay on in Allahabad, so Shyama and I joined the YWCA's newly opened hostel for college women on Lawrence Road. I now wonder why we never thought of asking someone we knew to escort me to college on the first day. Janak, who was already on staff at Lahore College for Women as a lecturer in English, escorted me to the college gate and described the general layout from the outside. She told me to take the main staircase, cross the library, which opened on another verandah, and from there find the History Department. Once there, I would be looked after by someone. I was extremely nervous. Gone were the sheltered surroundings of a women's college as I suddenly entered the world of young men. Little did I know of the trouble and turmoil fate had in store for me.

Hearing loud voices, I walked into the library, which seemed full of young men. There was a hushed silence. When I found my voice, I asked for the history staff room and was directed there. Thus began my life at Government College.

As the only woman in a class of twenty-five or thirty men, I led a lonely existence. The history staff room became my refuge. I hardly ever opened my mouth when I was there, but I am sure my presence in the staff room placed a strain on the professors, who could not laugh or joke with a student present. I walked behind the professor as he entered the classroom and sat on a chair near his table. During class, I was in full view of twenty-five to thirty pairs of eyes. When the lecture was over, I quietly walked out behind the professor.

Because I was a woman, I did not join in any of the college activities, although much later I wrote occasionally for the college magazine. My parents had bought me a bicycle and I had learned to ride it in Allahabad, but my hometown was a quiet, sleepy place compared to the hustle and bustle of Lahore. So I preferred to walk to college from Lawrence Road, passing through *Gol Bagh* [a park], although the distance was great.

I missed my friends and my active life in Kinnaird College. There was one intercollegiate lecture for both Forman Christian College students and Government College fifth- and sixth-year history students. At that time, I used to meet my friend Prem Lata Sudan, who was one year ahead of me in Kinnaird College and also studying for the master's in history from Government College. We used to sit together on the last bench in Forman Christian College and make up for lost time. But this companionship was short and fleeting, as we both had other lectures to attend.

For some reason, Shyama did not want to join Kinnaird College for her bachelor's degree, so she persuaded her close friend and classmate Joyce Sirajuddin to join Forman Christian College with her. Since there were no recreational activities at this YWCA hostel, Shyama and I joined the university extension lectures in French. We walked to the university every evening and did extremely well in the French examination. We had every intention of continuing our French lessons the following year, but events in the country overwhelmed us.

It was at this time that both Shyama and I joined the Lahore Student Union as ordinary members with my friend Bachi Setna, a postgraduate science student at Government College who was staying in the same hostel. The student union had been founded by Shaheed Bhagat Singh. He and his comrades Bhagwati Charan and Sukhdev Raj became famous because of the Lahore Conspiracy Case of 1927. When the student union was first founded, Bhagat Singh lectured to members on the lives of the Indian martyrs who had fought for freedom. By the time we joined this organization, it had lost all its revolutionary spirit and become the forum for humdrum debates and lectures. Abdul Majid Khan, a master's in English student at the Forman Christian College and one year ahead of me, was the President of the student union. To him I owe my initiation into active politics. The honor of revitalizing the Lahore Student Union to become the revolutionary organization envisaged by its founders later fell on my shoulders.

Punjab University used to organize excursion tours to places of interest in India for women attending various colleges. While at Kinnaird, we had traveled to Agra and Delhi and the Khewra salt mines. In 1928 the excursion was planned for Benares, Gaya, and Calcutta. In Calcutta, the Indian National Congress was to meet under the presidentship of Pandit Motilal. Usually these trips were not open to women studying in men's colleges, but we persuaded the authorities to let us go since we were still students. So Shyama and I went to Calcutta and were able to attend the Calcutta session of the Congress. It was a historic occasion, as Congress accepted dominion status as its goal for the country. Mother was there, so it was also a kind of family reunion.

In 1929 Mother returned to Lahore and rented part of a bungalow on Panj Mahal Road. Father left one of his cars for our use, so there was no more bicycling and walking for Shyama and me.

Netaji Subhash Chandra Bose had been invited to preside over the Second All-Punjab Student Conference to be held in Lahore in October 1929. Abdul Majid came to our house and asked me to chair the student reception committee. His invitation surprised me. Never before had a female student ventured to take such a bold step. And the situation was even more complicated, because I was a student at a government institution. Although I admired Netaji and would have loved to accept Abdul Majid's offer, the responsibility and consequences of the post made me hesitate. Desperately in need of advice, I could consult neither my mother nor my father, since Mother was on a trip to Bombay and Baroda, while Father was in Allahabad. I turned to my sister Janak, who advised me to accept it. When I pointed out that I was studying at Government College, she suggested we could draft a harmless welcome speech that the college authorities could not possibly object to. She finally persuaded me, and the speech was drafted. But what neither of us took into account was the fact that, as Chair of the reception committee, I would have to go to the railway station and welcome the President-elect, and then go around the city in a procession with him. Fortunately, an untoward incident occurred and the conference with its usual resolutions was a great success. My mother, receiving the news of the conference in Baroda where she was staying with Abbas Tayabji (an old family friend and a veteran Congress leader), hurried back to Lahore to see her daughter occupying an important position in this conference of young men. Back in Lahore, she gave a small tea party in honor of Subhash Chandra Bose.

I had assumed that the end of the conference would mark the conclusion of this relationship with the student association, but then Abdul Majid mentioned that it was conventional to elect the Chair of the reception committee as the new President. I protested in vain. Abdul Majid argued that he had become President in this way and that I had no choice but to accept.

Although I regard myself as having a retiring nature, I also have an irrepressible adventurous streak and so found myself the first woman President of the Lahore Student Union, which had a membership of about eight hundred. Before long, it became apparent that this step, taken so casually and lightheartedly, would involve me in the grim struggle for the country's freedom.

Because the student union had been founded by Bhagat Singh, the great revolutionary leader, it had earned government disapproval. The government could not ban it, however, as its activities were harmless. Becoming the President of such a body was tantamount to poking my fingers into the eyes of the authorities. My previous action—welcoming a Congress leader of the stature of Subhash Bose—was especially provocative for a student of Government College. Looking back, I feel that some power must have been guiding me as I conducted myself so that no action could be taken against me until I openly courted arrest by picketing my old college.

I was the head of the student union when the Indian National Congress held its historic session in Lahore in December 1929. At that session the resolution passed that the country's goal was complete independence. This session was presided over by Jawaharlal Nehru. The previous Calcutta session had passed a resolution that India would be content with dominion status under the British crown. It had been vehemently opposed by Jawaharlal, who had felt that nothing short of severing all ties with the British would satisfy the younger generation in the Congress. Credit goes to him for having persevered throughout 1929 to bring his senior colleagues to his way of thinking. Having attended the Calcutta session a year earlier, both Shyama and I were impressed with the role of women volunteers, so we signed up for the same duty at the Lahore session. While Calcutta women had the glamorous young leader Subhash Bose as their Commander-in-Chief, we had to make do with S. Mangal Singh as our General Officer in Command (GOC) and with Trilok Chand Kapur as his Deputy. Our own captain was Kumari Lajja Vati.

Long before the session was due to begin, we began vigorous training in marching. The instructor, Mr. Iyer, had come from the South. He was a member of the Hindustani Seva Dal, a volunteer corps attached to Congress. Since the annual session of Congress was a mammoth affair, it needed a large number of disciplined volunteers. Shyama and I, educated in a convent, knew what marching in step meant. So, after giving us preliminary training and satisfying himself that I could train the rest of the women, Mr. Iyer made me the instructor of the women's corps, while he devoted his attention to the training of the men. They formed a larger percentage of the volunteers and were also more varied in background. Unlike the women, they were recruited from different Punjabi districts and from different educational institutions. Hardly any of them could walk in step, so they really had to work hard to be able to march properly.

I never realized until then that I had learned to walk with a long stride. Unconsciously, that is how I taught the women under me to march, so when we had to go on long marches as a group I found the women out of step with the men, who took shorter steps. However, that was a minor problem and we enjoyed our long marches on those early cold winter mornings. Soon all was in readiness for the conference.

The Nehru family came a few days early and were guests of Lala Harkishan Lal, a noted Punjabi industrialist. Jawaharlal was also there. A small city of tents had been put up on the banks of the river Ravi. Delegates from all parts of the country began to arrive. Kitchens had been set up and *pandals* for various functions were ready. Volunteers, both men and women, who had come from outside the city, or those who wanted to live on the campus, were already in residence. All roads led to the Congress *nagar*. In our enclosure, Kumari Lajja Vati had already started to look after the women. Our uniform was an orange *khadi* sari with a green blouse. Officers, like Jai, Shakuntale, Shyama, and I, had been given leather belts with whistles and were very proud of ourselves. Since I was designated the Deputy Commander of our group, I had to assist Lajja Vati in her duties. We had all our meals with the volunteers except dinner, which we had with Pandit Motilal and other members of the family. As Mother had a number of duties and had to see to the last minute arrangements, she returned home very late at night. Shyama and I used to wait up for her. We were never bored. There were so many things to see and so many old and new friends to visit in the Congress *nagar* itself that we really had no time for anything else.

At last the great day arrived. Jawaharlal, who was already in Lahore, traveled to Amritsar (thirty-two miles away) to return to Lahore by the afternoon train so that he could be welcomed formally by the Punjab Provincial Congress Committee and taken around the city in a procession. The Punjabis, a martial race, had hit on the novel idea of making the President-elect ride a horse instead of taking him in a horse-drawn carriage or car. Earlier that morning there had been a little trouble with the male volunteers. The entire contingent could not be spared to escort the President-elect because of watch and ward duty. Only half of them were to proceed to the railway station. But so popular was Jawaharlal as a youth leader that the volunteers expressed their disappointment. On further inquiry, they were informed that 100 out of 107 of the young women would join the procession. The male volunteers then insisted that half of the young women should also be kept back. In vain, our GOC, Sardar Mangal Singh, explained that the total number of young women was very small and also that they had not been given such important and strenuous duties. But the young men would not listen. In the end, Kumari Lajja Vati and about 50 young women stayed back. She kept Shyama to assist her in looking after those left behind. I was sent to the station in charge of the depleted contingent. After an early lunch, we walked all the way to the railway station.

The train steamed in and the leaders welcomed the President-elect by presenting flower garlands while others shouted national slogans. Outside the station, everyone waited in readiness. The bands, cars to accompany the President-elect, riders to escort him, volunteers standing in the order in which they would have to march, all were facing the exit gate of the railway station so that as soon as the word of command was given, the whole procession could move forward. To harass us and throw us into confusion, the police suddenly switched the entrance and exit gates. The entrance to the railway station now became the exit. Although there was hardly room to move around, the procession had to be rearranged. The railway station and all roads leading to it were a seething mass of humanity.

There was so much noise and confusion that in the excitement I forgot that I was a volunteer in uniform and on duty. I was looking around with my back to the railway station, when someone gave me a playful pat on my cheeks. Startled, I turned around and found Jawahar Bhai (as I called him) standing next to me grumbling about the arrangements. The crowd was so large at the platform that in the pushing and jostling he was separated from the leaders and suddenly found himself standing near the women. However, everything was sorted out and the procession reassembled. The President-elect mounted his horse and we started off with bands playing and the crowds shouting national slogans. We moved slowly through the narrow streets of the city. I think we must have marched at least twenty miles that day. It was a gala day for the public. Hundreds had lined the streets to welcome Jawaharlal. The city was decorated with arches and buntings and he was showered with garlands and flowers.

The Servants of the People Society, a social welfare institution founded by Lala Lajpat Rai, had constructed an assembly hall. It was decided that the procession would terminate there so Jawaharlal could officially open the hall. The public who had walked with the procession went home and the male volunteers prepared to walk back to the camp. The women decided to walk with them. Because the road to Congress *nagar* was rather lonely, it was safer for us to accompany this large group of young men than to walk by ourselves. Later that night, when we reached our camp, we realized that we had had nothing to eat or drink since our early lunch. It was now after 7:00 P.M. and bitterly cold. When we were on duty, we were not permitted to wear coats or shawls. Dr. Gopi Chand, one of our local leaders, insisted that the women stay back because he had ordered the volunteer bus from the camp for us to go back in comfort. I protested that our present mood of excitement, walking another six or seven miles would be no hardship. He refused to let us go. I suppose he did not like the idea of a group of young men and women walking together without the supervision of an older person. On his insistence we stayed back and the young men left. Three of the male volunteers stayed back to protect us as we waited for the bus. Looking back now, I realize how important this gesture was as we waited amongst a crowd of strange men. At the time, I am afraid we failed to appreciate their sense of responsibility, although we did welcome the presence of those three young men.

The inaugural function concluded successfully and the guests went home. Jawaharlal also left after asking how we were all going home. Suddenly I noticed that a group of women, not officially part of the procession, were waiting in the hall. When I asked why they had not gone home, they replied that Dr. Gopi Chand had promised to see them home in the volunteer bus. I mentioned that our group of women volunteers was more than a bus load and that there would not be room for anyone else. They replied that they had waited a long time, their menfolk had gone home, and they intended to go in the bus regardless of what anyone said. The bus arrived and they all scrambled in. I was very upset that here I was, with more than fifty young women for whom I was responsible, and there was no bus. I was young myself, barely twenty years of age, and it was already quite late and dark. How would all of us get back to the camp? We were tired and hungry and longing for our dinner. It would be ages before the bus returned after dropping these women home, as the streets were narrow and crowded. So I asked the driver to wait while I went to the society's residential quarters to look for Dr. Gopi Chand. I found him sitting comfortably before a charcoal fire, warmly clad in a shawl and eating his dinner. I explained the situation to him and asked him to make other arrangements for those women so that we could return to the camp as soon as possible where our parents would be waiting and worrying.

He replied that it would not take very long for those women to be dropped off first. They had walked in the procession, he said, and deserved consideration. I retorted that the whole city had come with us; were we responsible for seeing them all home? Why could not the bus, meant for the volunteers, drop us off first and then return to take these other women home? He would not listen and said we could all go in the next trip. I was so incensed that I told him I did not need his help but would make arrangements for the women volunteers myself.

The bus left. I divided the young women into groups of four, depending on where they lived, and sent them home in *tongas*. Dr. Gopi Chand finished his dinner and left in the car, leaving his wife and daughter Rukmini behind. Not living there and not knowing what to do or how they were going to get back to the camp, they came and joined us. Everyone had left except Jai, Shiva, me, and the three young men. So now there were eight of us, all waiting for some sort of transport.

Fortunately, Jawaharlal, who had been dining with Lala Harkishan Lal, came over with Pandit K. Santanam (one of our local leaders) and S.D. Upadhyaya, who was Pandit Motilal's private secretary in those days. Some suspicion that all might not have gone well made Jawaharlal tell Santanam that he wanted to visit the Servants of the People Society's hall before proceeding to the Congress *nagar*. Santanam protested that there would be no one there at that time of night, but Jawaharlal insisted. When he came, he found us shivering in the cold, tired, hungry, and angry. Hearing the whole story, he was very upset and asked three of us to go with him. But we were not prepared to leave our companions, and there was no room in the car for all eight of us. I persuaded him to take Mrs. Gopi Chand and Rukmini with him and send some sort of transport for the rest of us immediately. Seeing that we had no warm clothing he took off his overcoat and asked me to put it on. Santanam and Upadhyaya did the same so that at least Jai, Shiva, and I had warm coats. Finally a car arrived, and we reached the camp long after 11:00 P.M.

The next morning I related this incident to the rest of the women. Kumari Lajja Vati had already been apprised of all the details by her sister Shiva. At my suggestion, the women decided to go on strike unless Dr. Gopi Chand came in person and apologized. Although Lajja Vati was angry about the incident, she tried to calm us down by arguing that the formal session of Congress was about to begin and we could not let Congress down. But we were adamant. Our GOC, Sardar Mangal Singh, came and apologized, but it had no effect. Finally Dr. Gopi Chand arrived looking very sheepish because he had already been reprimanded by Jawaharlal. He apologized and we resumed our duties.

The two or three of us who were college students were placed on duty at the Subjects Committee *pandal*. Lajja Vati hoped we would be interested in the discussion and that our knowledge of the country's affairs would increase. But I was too far from the dais and there was so much coming and going that I kept losing the thread of the discussion. Finally, I gave up the attempt to listen and started talking to people loitering near the entrance. Since most of these people were from the South, we conversed in English. One Punjabi gentleman standing at the back was listening with great interest. Later on he asked me when I had learned to speak English and on hearing that I was a student studying for my master's degree his surprise knew no bounds. It seemed he had left India about twenty-five or thirty years earlier to settle in the United States. When he left, women were more or less in *purdah*, and hardly any girls attended school. To see so many young women walking about freely in the Congress *nagar* was an eye-opener. Whenever he saw me off-duty, he discussed with me the changes he saw in India and in particular those affecting women. When I told him that many young women were not only in school but at the university, he was amazed.

When the main Congress session started, one group of women, including Shyama, was in the choir that sang a specially composed opening song. Mother had asked a Muslim friend, Mr. Bashir Ahmed, to write it for the occasion.

The Congress *pandal* was a huge place divided into various sections for different categories of visitors. The women's enclosure was very large. I was posted at the main women's gate with three or four other women to check tickets; the rest were posted at various strategic points to escort the women to their seats and generally look after them. Several of the women brought their children. First, many women had nowhere and no one with whom to leave their children. Second, they felt that children also need an outing. Whatever the reason, the female volunteers had to see that the children did not cry or make noise and disturb the proceedings. Believe me, it would have been far less arduous to be on duty at the main gate. Besides checking tickets and passing the women visitors on to the female volunteers inside, I had to cope with a horde of men who appeared with eatables and a request that I pass them on to their womenfolk. I pleaded that I was busy punching tickets and that I had no idea who accompanied whom, but it was useless. The demands continued. The men could not understand why I was unable to identify their womenfolk, and I could not make them understand why the women should have eaten before coming in to attend the session. After all, they were aware that it was not a fair but a serious session where the country's leaders had gathered to chalk out plans for India's future. But when all was said and done, it was great fun and we enjoyed ourselves thoroughly.

That Congress session was a landmark in my life, and subsequent events happened because of it. My sister and I were living at home and had to be at our camp, at least ten miles from home, by 7:00 A.M. sharp. We had our camp flag hoisting ceremony at 7:30 A.M., so we would be free to join in the general flag-hoisting ceremony at the

Congress *nagar* at 8:00 A.M. This flag was lowered at 6:00 P.M., and a little later the same ceremony was repeated at our camp. There were special songs for both these occasions that men and women sang together. The national anthem was not the same then as it is now. In those days, "*Vande Mataram*" was considered the national anthem.

Generally, after the flag was lowered, we were free unless there was a late session of the Subjects Committee. Since there was so much activity in the *nagar* after on-duty hours, we young women used to loiter around visiting various camps and talking to people. The male volunteers had a much harder task, as they worked throughout the twenty-four hours in shifts. But no one grudged this hard work. It was a new experience and we never had a dull moment. The exhibition grounds were also our special field of duty, but on the very first day one of the visitors shook hands with one of the young women on duty. In fact, these visitors were going the wrong way, and when the volunteer put out her hand to prevent their doing so, one of them clasped her hand. Whether it was intentional or a joke we never knew, but the incident was taken seriously and the exhibition was declared out of bounds for us. Now, as soon as the main Congress session was over, we were free. Most of the young women went home. We could not visit the exhibition even after on-duty hours until we begged Captain Lajja Vati to lift the ban. Finally, she relented.

At the Congress *nagar* it was impressed on all volunteers, male and female alike, that under no circumstances were we to let any of the All-India leaders, particularly Gandhiji, enter any meetings or exhibitions until we had checked their passes. This was to be followed very strictly where Gandhiji was concerned because that was his method of checking whether the volunteers had been properly trained. Usually everyone gave way to him with folded hands. Mindful of this rule, my sister Shyama once stopped him and requested his pass. The people surrounding him were horrified. How dare she insult Mahatma Gandhi! Did she not realize who he was? Shyama said she knew him very well but would not let him enter until he showed her his pass. He remarked that he had forgotten it in his camp, but since she knew him would she not relax the rule in his favor? Shyama said she would send a volunteer to fetch his pass but without checking it she was sorry, but she could not let him in. He chuckled at that and produced his card. He said he was only testing the efficiency of the volunteers. At the end of the three-day session the volunteer corps, and especially the young women, received high praise from the leaders for their discipline, courtesy, and good behavior.

It was at this time, on December 23, 1929, that Kiren Chandra Das, brother of the well-known revolutionary Jatin Das of the Lahore Conspiracy Case, together with Comrades Ram Kishan, Dhanwantry Virindra, and three others, was arrested at the Congress *nagar*. Since the police were forbidden to enter the camp, they informed the local high command of their presence and their reason for being there. We all gathered around Kiren Das and his friends and escorted them to the gate, where they were formally handed over to the police. Their arrest was in connection with the viceregal "train outrage" (as it was called) in Delhi. A bomb had been thrown onto the Viceroy's train as it passed under *Purana Qila* [the Old Fort]. No one was hurt. The attack had been organized by the two revolutionaries Yashpal and Bhagwati Charan. Kiran Das and his companions were released after two months of detention as the director of the intelligence bureau was honest enough to admit that he had no clear proof that they had committed the act.

The Subjects Committee focused its discussion on the methods of rejuvenating the struggle for freedom. According to Gandhi, the country was ready for it. There was a small tax on salt that was a hardship to the poor as most of them could not afford vegetables or *dal* [lentils] and would eat only dry *roti* [bread] with salt. For them, even a small tax on salt was too much. Gandhiji had decided to launch an attack on this. He outlined a plan that was designed to be both simple and effective. He would walk from Sabarmati ashram in Ahmadabad to a tiny village called Dandi in the state of Maharashtra. This would, in his opinion, provide the necessary spark for a nationwide *satyagraha* movement. This famous 388-kilometer march, which began on March 12, 1930, has been called the most brilliant political challenge of modern times. It took Gandhiji and his party twenty-four days to complete. At Dandi, amidst the chanting of hymns and shouting of national slogans, Gandhiji broke the Salt Law on April 6, 1930. He walked a little way into the sea, picked up some salt from the salt pans, and so defied the Salt Law.

For the first time in the history of the country's fight for freedom, a day was fixed to be celebrated as Independence Day. That day, January 26, was to be celebrated annually with the recitation of the following pledge:

> We believe that it is the inalienable right of the Indian people, as any other people, to have freedom and to enjoy the fruits of their toil and have the necessities of life, so that they may have full opportunities of growth. We believe also that if any Government deprives a people of these rights and oppresses them, the people have a further right to alter it or to abolish it. The British Government in India has not only deprived the Indian people of their freedom, but has based itself on the exploitation of the masses, and has ruined India economically, politically, culturally, and spiritually. We believe, therefore, that India must sever the British connection and attain *puran swaraj*, or complete independence.

This pledge, which framed the expression of our political ideas, was a far cry from the home rule movement of Lokmanya Tilak in the 1920s and the acceptance of dominion status in 1928.

5

The *Satyagraha* Movement

The first Independence Day, January 26, 1930, came around soon after the Lahore Congress session, and it was the celebration of this event that brought the Lahore Student Union and me into conflict with the college authorities. Hundreds of national flags were sold openly in the city, and people displayed them boldly. University students enthusiastically welcomed this day and proudly wore the national flag on the lapels of their coats. For the first time, people began to recognize a flag different from the Union Jack. The students of Maclagan Engineering College in Mughulpura (a suburb of Lahore) were no exception. While the authorities at other colleges ignored this gesture of defiance, the Maclagan College authorities decided on a different course. One of the professors, an Englishman, took offense at this blatant expression of sympathy with Congress, fined the students, and expelled them from his class. In sympathy with their fellow students, the entire college went on strike. They sent word to the Lahore Student Union asking for support.

The officers and active members of the student union reported the matter to me and suggested that we all go to Maclagan College to find out the details and see if the strike could be settled amicably. I was a little hesitant since it would be my first experience of going to a men's college other than my own. When we met the students, they were in a nasty temper. They felt their expulsion was an insult to the national flag. The principal was away but returned immediately. Meanwhile, we met the vice-principal. After a great deal of talking and many meetings with local Congress leaders, a compromise was effected, and the authorities agreed to three of the four demands of the students, including cancellation of the fine.

The principal was a very broad-minded man so the strike was amicably settled. Together with my colleagues in the Lahore Student Union, I was invited for tea at Stiffles restaurant in Lahore by the Engineering College students. My mother, who was always very liberal, permitted me to attend a party where I was the only young woman among many young men.

While the students of the Engineering College were happy with their victory, I still had much to face. The principal of my college, Mr. H.L.O. Garrett, had taken a long leave of absence. The officiating principal, Dr. H.B. Dunnicliffe, head of the Chemistry Department, was well known for his anti-Indian views. On learning of the part I played in the Maclagan Engineering College affair, he decided to make an example of me. I was asked to meet him in his office to explain my conduct. On my inquiring whether anyone from the Maclagan Engineering College had complained, he replied in the negative. On the contrary, he said that the principal had nothing but the highest praise for me. But he asked me to resign from the Lahore Student Union. I pointed out that our activities were not directed against the government. I also mentioned that my intervention ended a conflict which could well have developed into a major conflagration affecting other colleges as well. I suggested that he ban the student union instead, but he would not listen. He believed it was the duty of a student to obey the principal. I was equally determined not to resign, so an impasse was created. What the principal did not realize was that I had been brought up in the atmosphere of Congress and the national movement was very much in my blood. Seeing my attitude, he mellowed a little. He asked me to go home, consult my parents, and come and see him in a few days. When I told my mother about this meeting, she consulted Pandit K. Santanam, who in turn sought the advice of Bakshi Tek Chand, one of the eminent judges of the Punjab High Court. Bakshiji was of the opinion that, instead of going to see the principal, I should write a letter to him reiterating what I had said earlier: that I would not resign from the student union and that, if he thought fit, the entire organization could be declared illegal by the government. I followed this advice and sent the letter. Bakshiji felt that if we had to contest any order of the principal in a court of law, we should have something in writing. My father was already studying the Punjab University Act with the intention of taking legal action against the university in case they expelled me without just cause. The principal's anger was something that needed to be seen to be believed. He was so angry that I had dared to write a letter when he had ordered me to come and see him in person that he was ready for drastic action. My master's degree final examination was only two months away, and it would have been a great blow if after completing all that hard work and even submitting my thesis I were debarred from sitting for the final examination.

Fortunately for all concerned, the head of the English Department, Professor Langhorne, prevailed upon Dr. Dunnicliffe to let me continue my studies. He pointed out the absurdity of expelling a woman from a men's educational institution for political reasons on the eve of the *satyagraha* movement. Who knew what the future would be? The Indians might win their freedom. What reply would the college give to the Independent Central Assembly (as the parliament was then called) should they be put to the mat? If I failed, the college could always refuse me readmission. In any case, "preparatory leave" would start very soon and I would no longer be attending lectures. We came to know of Professor Langhorne's suggestions through the Indian members of the staff. I had been asked by my advisers to continue attending all lectures and refuse to quit unless the principal ordered me to in writing. Finally, Dr. Dunnicliffe conceded and no drastic action was taken.

By God's good grace I passed my examination, so there was no need to tax the generosity of the college authorities. Because of this incident, I gained a certain amount of publicity, and, wherever I went, there were groups of students standing around to talk with me. Letters from Dr. Dunnicliffe would be delivered to me by groups of two or three students. I was mystified as to why the college peon did not deliver them until I discovered that Dr. Dunnicliffe's practice was to hand his letters to any student he saw standing outside his office with the injunction to deliver it to me. The students used to steam the letters open, read them, reseal them, and then come to my house to hand them over to me.

They were also greatly intrigued by the exchange, since no other woman had ever been asked to meet with the principal. Whenever I was summoned, there was always a crowd of students loitering outside the principal's office.

But there had been other occasions when I was singled out for special attention. When I joined Government College, I had asked my father to send my fees directly to the college from Allahabad by money order. On one occasion he had to go out of town on a case and forgot to send my fees for a particular month. I knew nothing about it until one fine morning Mr. Garrett announced to the entire class that I had ceased to be a student of the college as my fees for that particular month had not been paid. If I wanted to remain in college and continue my studies, I would have to pay the admission fee a second time. I was stunned, and my classmates were flabbergasted. Perhaps he was hoping that my father would refuse to pay the admission fee a second time and the college would be well rid of a rebel like me. But when he arrived back in Allahabad and received my letter, my father promptly sent the admission fee and the late fee, so the authorities could not do anything. When the principal, Mr. Garrett, announced this my classmates were shocked. They crowded around me in the corridor after class expressing their surprise. They expected a female student to be treated with more consideration. Most of them said that they paid their fees only twice a year and no action had ever been taken against them. What could I say? I knew and they knew that this was punishment for my flouting of college norms. Not only had I welcomed a Congress leader like Netaji Subhas Bose, but I had actively participated in the Congress session of 1929 by becoming a volunteer.

I well remember how difficult it was to study in those days. At the Lahore session of the Congress, Gandhiji had explained that once the Salt Law had been defied the Congress could break any other law by peaceful means. But it was necessary to start the *satyagraha* movement by breaking the Salt Law. A number of top leaders were hesitant. How could the movement start with such a small symbolic gesture? Gandhiji's march would not have any effect on the British Government! But Gandhiji knew how small things could lead to bigger ones, and that was exactly what happened.

Gandhiji's march from Ahmadabad to the little village of Dandi launched the biggest movement in the anals of any slave country of the world. It was expected that all Congress committees would defy the Salt Law, even if there were no sea or river water available. My mother and the other Congress leaders of the Punjab were in a dilemma. Where were we to start the *satyagraha* movement? There was no sea in the Punjab, which was known as the land of the five rivers.

It so happened that Jawaharlal stopped at Lahore on his way to Gujarat to preside over a political conference. He took the leaders to task for not having done anything to start the *satyagraha* movement. When they explained the problem, he replied that even well water would suffice. After all, no one really thought the British government would repeal the Salt Law because a handful of people had tried to manufacture salt by boiling sea water. This was only a gesture of defiance. We had the river Ravi; what were we waiting for? he asked. Immediately, preparations for breaking the Salt Law were begun. I have no recollection of the date, but I distinctly remember the huge crowd that gathered at Baradari (an old monument dating from Mughal days) on the banks of the Ravi on this fateful day. The water was collected from the river and poured into an enormous frying pan on a charcoal stove. The crowd waited patiently as if something wonderful were about to happen. When the water began to boil, the enthusiasm of the waiting crowd knew no bounds. Everyone was pushing just to have a glimpse of the boiling water. All the top leaders, including my mother, were standing around this huge stove despite the intense heat. They were so excited that I do not think they were even conscious of the heat. Finally, all the water evaporated and the sediment remaining was declared salt. Bits of it were reverently wrapped and auctioned for fantastic sums. I bought a tiny packet and gave it due honor and respect by keeping it on the mantelpiece of our drawing room in Panj Mahal Road for many months. Although my final master's examination was only a few days away, and Shyama was appearing for her bachelor's final, both of us attended this historic function. My married sister was visiting at the time, and she thought it madness the way Shyama and I were going about. She protested at the lighthearted manner in which I was studying. I explained to her that the examinations were held every year and that if I failed this time, I could sit for it again, but that evening at Baradari would never be repeated again.

The *satyagraha* movement was launched after this. All Congress committees throughout the Punjab organized meetings and processions and the picketing of foreign cloth and liquor shops. I had not yet started taking an active part as I was waiting for the examination to be over, but I would sit for hours in the verandah of our house on Panj

Mahal Road planning the students' participation in the Congress programs. Once the ordeal of the examinations was over, I was free to attend meetings and processions and participate in the picketing of shops, which was left to the women. Women were considered less likely to retaliate in anger should some incident occur.

One particular picketing incident stands out in my mind. A group of women were picketing the shop of R.S. Bhola Ram and Sons (wine merchants) and a crowd had collected. Whatever we did inside the walled city had no impact on the society people of Lahore, but R.S. Bhola Ram was the biggest wine shop in Lahore and was situated in a posh locality, and picketing it was bound to attract more attention. Looking back, I wonder if picketing was the right thing to do. These were our countrymen, and they had invested large amounts of money in their businesses. The British never suffered—only the Indians—and many of them had genuine sympathy for our cause and secretly helped us.

When a whole row of shops was to be picketed, two volunteers were assigned to each shop. It was tedious work since the shopkeepers offered no resistance. They would neither call the police to throw us out nor threaten to have us arrested, so there was no excitement. Often, I would take along my *takli* [flat, needlelike instrument] and start spinning cotton yarn. It was not that the yarn would ever be of any use, but this activity helped pass the time. We knew that picketing a few shops once in a while could not affect the trade with England. All it meant was that the shopkeeper would not earn anything that day. I do not know why Gandhiji never thought of the hardships picketing imposed on petty traders. Rich merchants like R.S. Bhola Ram and Sons were hardly affected at all.

Before Congress passed the Independence resolution in 1929, they knew that stern action would be taken against them by the government. After arresting the all-India leaders, the government was expected to ban all Congress committees and arrest all officebearers. The movement would be paralyzed before it could affect the general masses. Predicting that this would happen, the Congress Working Committee disbanded all Congress committees. A list of all-India Dictators was drawn up. The original list was secret, but each Dictator knew who his successor was to be, so that at the time of his arrest the next Dictator could be informed. When Maulana Abul-Kalam Azad was arrested in Delhi in May 1930, he nominated my mother, Mrs. Lado

Rani Zutshi, to succeed him as the next all-India Dictator. Mrs. Sarojini Naidu was in Bombay and for some reason had not been arrested. When she heard about my mother she protested that as a member of the Congress Working Committee it was her right to succeed Maulana Azad. We had to send a special messager to Delhi to see Maulana Abul Azad in the district jail to clarify the position. He reiterated that he had nominated my mother and that Mrs. Naidu's turn would come later. Believe me, being an all-India Dictator was no bed of roses. It only meant that the gates of prison were waiting.

Together with the local Congress leaders, Mother prepared a scheme for picketing the Central Legislative Assembly at Simla on the opening day. The whole plan was kept a secret. The Simla Congress Committee was given the task of working out the details. Four women from Lahore went: myself as leader, my sister Shyama, and two of our friends, Shakuntala and Avinash. Six women came from Ambala, and the rest were drawn from Simla itself. Altogether, we were twenty-seven women. The resourceful President of the Simla Congress Committee, Dr. N.L. Varma, had organized it so well that we were sent in batches of twos and threes to assemble at the front of the Central Assembly building. We were to wave black flags and shout "Go back, Irwin." Lord Irwin was then the Viceroy of India and was going to inaugurate the monsoon session of the Assembly. Soon we were a goodly number. Dr. Verma came in a ricksha with curtains drawn so that he would not be seen, but so that he could be there to boost our morale.

A few people were loitering about outside, but there were no crowds. It is surprising that the strangeness of a group of women standing there quietly, neither entering the building nor walking away, struck an Indian policeman and not the Anglo-Indian sergeant on duty. The policeman drew the sergeant's attention to this strange phenomenon, and the sergeant came up to inquire what we were doing. On my replying that we were merely standing there, he asked us to move either across the road or to the side of the steps, as the Viceroy, the Commander-in-Chief, and the Governor of the Punjab would all be arriving and that particular space would be needed for parking their cars. I had never been to Simla before and was unaware that, standing as we were, the Viceroy's car would face us and he would be bound to see us. It was sheer stubbornness that made us refuse to move from that spot. Time was very short. It was already 2:45 P.M. and the Viceroy was due to arrive punctually at 3:00 P.M. Our refusal to move was the first inkling the police had that we were not there for pleasure. The Assembly chamber had no extra police, and no car was permitted on the roads, so how could extra police be brought in? They would have to come from the nearest police station on the mall, and it would take at least fifteen minutes. Meanwhile, the Viceroy would have arrived. The police were in a fix. With great difficulty, they were able to muster five policemen, who tried to throw a cordon around us. But how could five men hide a group of twenty-seven women from the Viceroy? The sergeant kept on shouting, "Push them back!" while the Viceroy's car drove up. We promptly drew out the black flags hidden in the folds of our saris and shouted "Irwin, go back." You can imagine the furor it created! Lord Irwin got down from his car and walked up the steps to the Assembly chamber in a dignified manner. He never showed that he had seen or heard us. But there is a window overlooking the main road, and Lord Irwin was only human. He paused for a while on his way up to look down on the demonstration against him.

After he was inside, there was no point to our shouting ourselves hoarse. We formed a small procession and marched to the mall, singing national songs and shouting slogans. Never in the history of the summer capital of the British Empire had a handful of women been able to defy law and order so successfully. It was the first time that a procession had been taken out on the mall. The authorities were stunned and failed to take any action against us. Several inquiries were instituted as to how Congress had been able to plan a successful demonstration against the Viceroy. I am sure a large number of officers must have been transferred. We were, of course, jubilant. Four of us stayed in Simla for ten days and visited the Indian members of the Assembly at their residences and asked them to resign. I do not think it had the slightest effect on those seasoned politicians, but they liked to have four attractive young girls visit them every morning. We were always made welcome and entertained with a cup of tea or breakfast. That is how I met Sri M.R. Jayakar the first time. He and Sir Tej Bahadur Sapru were moderate leaders who believed in cooperating with the British Government. Mr. Jayakar and I became good friends and continued to meet after I was married and my husband was posted in Bombay.

This action of Congress created a stir in the country. Everything had been kept so secret that even my father in Allahabad knew nothing about it. As the accounts of this demonstration were published in the newspapers, he wrote and asked Mother if these Zutshi girls were his daughters or did they belong to some other family of the same name?

Soon after we returned from Simla, Mother was arrested. So far the Punjab government had refrained from arresting women, but Mother was an all-India Dictator. She could not be left outside for long. As it was, she had enjoyed a respite of two or three months, but rumors of her imminent arrest had been afloat for a long time. Even so, her arrest was most unexpected. It was August 1930. I had returned from a public meeting and was having a late dinner out on the lawn. Some friends had taken Mother out for a drive in their car, and my sisters Janak and Shyama were inside the house. All of a sudden, I looked up and saw the police standing in front of me. It was past midnight. They had left their car parked outside the gate and had walked up so softly that I did not hear their footsteps. They inquired if Mother was in, though I am certain that they knew through their Criminal Investigation Department (CID) that she was not. On my replying that she had gone out, they said they would wait. I hurriedly finished my dinner, ran inside, and told my sisters that the police had come for Mother. They rushed out to see the posse of police sent to arrest one lone woman who was fighting peacefully for her country's freedom.

Mother returned before long and was taken away by the police. As she was a prisoner awaiting trial, she was entitled to food from home. The next morning when we took her breakfast to the Lahore Female Jail, we found to our dismay that she was not there. We were worried as to where she could be, but nobody would give us any information. After a search of all the police stations we finally found her, at midnight, at the Delhi Gate *Kotwali* (the largest police station) in a condemned prisoner's cell. The magistrate in charge of her case had forgotten to classify her. This meant further discomfort and harassment for her. It also meant that, until she could be classified, she would be treated like an ordinary criminal. We went to the magistrate's office but discovered that he had gone away and was not expected back for a couple of days. Fortunately, we were able to approach the district magistrate, Mr. Edgar Lewis; the mistake was rectified, and Mother was transferred to the Lahore Female Jail and placed in class A. Subsequently, she was sentenced to one year of simple imprisonment. As she was an all-India Dictator and a well-known figure in the social and political circles of Lahore, her arrest created a sensation. As a rule, women were not being arrested in northern India. She was the first. Srimati Pooran Devi was arrested in September 1930 and placed in class B. Mother's trial was held in a big hall in the jail hospital compound. Father had come from Allahabad for the trial and attended it with several of our relatives and friends and local Congress workers.

After Mother's imprisonment, we settled down to a life of meetings and processions. The most exciting event for us was the raid by the police in the early hours of one morning when Janak, Shyama, and I were fast asleep. Because it was still summer we were sleeping on the lawn. The raid was in connection with the *Peshawar Inquiry Committee Report* published by the Congress. It so happened that in April 1930, the Second Battalion of the Eighteenth Garhwal Rifles was stationed in Peshawar. Those were the days when the *satyagraha* movement had caught the imagination of the people. The Salt Law was defied everywhere, and large-scale arrests were taking place. On April 23, when Congress workers of Peshawar had been arrested and were being escorted to prison, a large crowd collected and soon became violent. The Garhwal Battalion was called out to fire on the mob, but they only followed this order much later. The next day the platoon commander was punished for slackness. The battalion was disarmed and moved to Havelian, a small town in the North West Frontier Province. There they were court-martialed and sentenced to various terms ranging from three years' imprisonment to transportation.

Naturally, there was a wave of resentment in the country against such high-handedness. The Working Committee of the Congress appointed an inquiry committee with Vithal Bhai Patel as Chair and Ranjit Pandit as Secretary. Their findings were published in a book called the *Peshawar Inquiry Committee Report*, which was banned by the government. Mother had been asked to sell a few copies, and a parcel containing the report had been posted to the address of a friend living in the neighborhood. If it had come directly to our address, it would have been confiscated immediately. One afternoon, my sister Janak put the books in the car, drove around, and sold them to various friends whom we had contacted earlier. In her excitement, she forgot to save a copy for us. I was very upset and protested, but nothing could be done. Finally, I got a copy of the report from our landlord's son, who lived in the other half of the house. I read the book until late at night, then put it on the bedside table. At 5:00 A.M., the police arrived with the friend who had originally received the parcel. It appears that they had gone to his house first. He pacified them by informing them of the real culprits and brought them to our house. Since they had a search warrant, we opened the house for them. Suddenly, I saw the book lying in full view of the police. I hurriedly picked it up, hid it in the folds of my sari, and gave it to the servant to return to the landlord's son.

The police did not have the faintest idea what the report looked like—its size, its thickness, whether it was hardbound or had a soft cover, or anything else about it. During the search they found an old locked trunk. They demanded the keys, and we said we had no idea where they were. In fact, the trunk contained only odds and ends and had been locked by Mother. We had no idea what it contained or where the keys were. The police became suspicious and broke open the lock. We were horrified to find two volumes of *Bharat Mein Augrezi Raj* [British Rule in India] in Hindi by Sunder Lal. This was another proscribed book that Mother had bought and safely hid. The discovery of it came as a great shock to us, and we believed that all three of us would be arrested there and then. We dared not say anything or even look at each other. But the police had no idea what it was, so they put the books back in the trunk. Since the *Peshawar Inquiry Committee Report* had not been found, they left.

All that was happening was related to events which had begun in 1928 when the British appointed a commission with Sir John Simon as its Chair. Simon was to tour India and formulate a proposal for the next stage of representative government. The terms of the commission were not very hopeful, so Congress had asked the public to boycott it and hold demonstrations against it. When the commission arrived in Lahore in March 1928, a huge demonstration was organized at the railway station, headed by our veteran leader, "The Lion of the Punjab," Lala Lajpat Rai. The police *lathi*-charged the crowd, and one of them hit Lalaji so hard that he never recovered from the blow. He suffered internal injuries and passed away on November 17, 1928.

The revolutionaries did not believe in Gandhiji's creed of nonviolence. They vowed vengeance on the senior superintendent of police at Lahore, an Englishman named J.A. Scott, who had ordered the assault on Lala Lajpat Rai. A plan was masterminded by Chandra Shekhar Azad, Bhagat Singh, and Raj Guru. They studied Scott's movements so surreptiously that the police had no inkling that he was under surveillance. Having laid their plans well, the revolutionaries decided that on the afternoon of December 17, 1928, Scott would be shot dead just as he was coming out of his office to go for lunch. Unfortunately, it was not Scott who came out of the police headquarters at this time, but his Deputy, J.P. Saunders. Saunders was shot dead on the spot by Raj Guru. The authorities immediately began arresting people all over the Punjab, but Chandra Shekhar Azad slipped away in the garb of a holy man and Bhagat Singh as a passenger in a first-class compartment accompanied by Durga Bhagwati Charan and her son. They eluded the police. The revolutionaries, calling themselves the Hindustan Republican Army, felt the country needed socialism to solve its economic problems. Under the new leadership of Chandra Shekhar Azad and Bhagat Singh, the name of the party was changed to the Hindustan Socialist Republican Association. In 1928, Bhagat Singh went to Calcutta to attend the Indian National Congress session held under the presidency of Pandit Motilal. He took this opportunity to persuade Jatin Das to teach some of the members of his group how to make bombs. Subsequently, Jatin Das moved to Agra. On April 8, 1929, Bhagat Singh and B.K. Dutt threw two bombs manufactured by Jatin Das into the Assembly hall at Delhi. At the same time, they threw copies of the "Red Leaflet."

The leaflet declared that this was an act ordered by the Hindustan Socialist Republic Army and, as I recall, concluded:

> Let the representatives of the people return to their constituencies and prepare the masses for the coming revolution, and let the Government know that while protesting against the Public Safety and Trades Dispute Bills and the callous murder of Lala Lajpat Rai on behalf of the Indian masses, we want to emphasize the lesson often repeated by history that it is easy to kill individuals, but you cannot kill ideas. Great empires crumbled while ideas survived. Bourbons and czars fell.
>
> We are sorry to admit that we who attach so great a sanctity to human life, we who dream of a glorious future, when man will be enjoying perfect peace and full liberty, have been forced to shed human blood. But the sacrifice of individuals at the altar of the great revolution that will bring freedom to all, rendering the exploitation of man by man impossible, is inevitable.

Neither of the two young men ran away. They waited in the visitor's gallery until the police arrived to arrest them. The bombs had been thrown so that they did no harm to anyone, but pandemonium broke out and members ran here and there. Pandit Motilal, a member of the Central Legislative Assembly, shouted to his colleagues not to run away because the young men were their own kith and kin. This came to be the famous Lahore Conspiracy Case.

Until this time the government had refused the revolutionaries' demands to be classified as political prisoners. All of those arrested were considered revolutionaries and treated as criminals. These young men demanded better treatment, amenities like newspapers and reading and writing materials, better food, and frequent visits with relations. Criminals were allowed only one visit and one letter every three months. They had to wear the regulation prison uniforms and eat prison food. Because the government refused their demands, Bhagat Singh and B.K. Dutt began a hunger strike in August 1929 to get special treatment in the Central Jail.

Bhagat Singh's comrades in the Lahore Conspiracy Case joined this hunger strike after thirty days. The condition of Jatin Das deteriorated very fast and became so precarious that the British Government prepared to release him before trial. But Jatin Das would not agree. By September 7 he had gone into a coma. I remember our anxious moments waiting to hear about his condition. We used to stand outside the gates of the Borstal Jail until late at night waiting for news. Toward the end, his brother, Kiren Chandra Das, was allowed to be near him and help in the nursing, but nothing could save him. Jatin Das died on September 13, 1929, at 12:55 P.M., after fasting for sixty-three days. He became a martyr in the country's fight for freedom. We were all there to pay homage to him as his body was brought out and taken through the streets in a procession. Subhash Chandra Bose had sent money, on behalf of the citizens of Calcutta, to bring the body to Calcutta by train. There the last rites were performed before a mammoth gathering of six hundred thousand people. This was the largest gathering Calcutta had witnessed since the death of the highly esteemed political leader Chittaranjan Das.

This hunger strike brought to the attention of the public the distinctions made between European and Indian prisoners. A wave of anger and shock ran the length and breadth of the country. The British Government realized they had gone too far in their callousness and indifference to the demands of political prisoners. In response, they amended the jail rules. Henceforth, pretrial prisoners, whatever their social status, could wear their own clothes. They could also get their food from home until the trial was over and they had been classified. All class A and B political prisoners were given one *thali* [plate], one *katori* [bowl], one glass, one *lota*, and one spoon, all of cheap aluminum. The class C prisoners were provided with one iron plate, nine or ten inches in diameter, called a *tasla*, and a small *katori*, but no glass or spoon. All cooking utensils and firewood were provided by the jail authorities. These regulations were to have a significant impact on our lives.

Janak Rani Tikku (1866–1880).
Mother of Lado Rani; wife of
Jeevan Lal Tikku.

Lado Rani Tikku Zutshi (1882–1968).

Ladli Prasad Zutshi (1875–1954).

The Four Zutshi Girls, c. 1916. From the left: Manmohini (7), Chandra (12), Shyama (5), Janak (10).

Motilal Nehru with Lado Rani and her four daughters, c. 1918. From the left: Chandra Zutshi, Krishna Nehru, Motilal Nehru, Lado Rani Zutshi, Shyama Zutshi, Manmohini Zutshi, Janak Zutshi.

Chandra Zutshi, M.A. graduation, 1925.

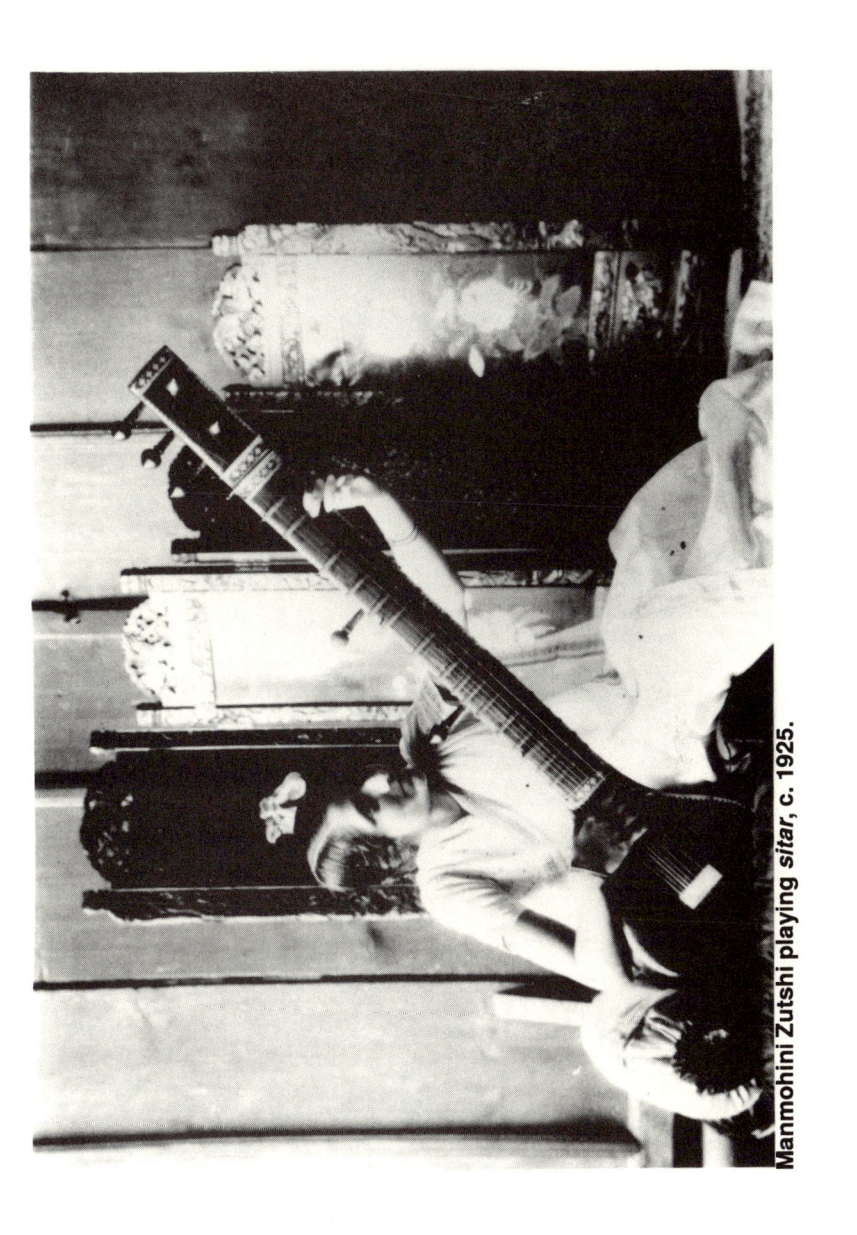

Manmohini Zutshi playing *sitar*, c. 1925.

Janak (standing) and Shyama (seated) Zutshi, c. 1926.

Jawaharlal Nehru

Vijayalaksmi Nehru Pandit, "With love."

Krishna Nehru (Hutheesingh) and her friend, Geneva, Switzerland 30 August, 1926.
Caption: "Helen (of Troy) and Krishna"

Subhas Chandra Bose, Students Conference, Lahore, 1929.

Mahatma Gandi, Karachi Congress, 1931.

A flying adventure, Karachi Congress, 1931. From left: a cousin, Indira Nehru (Gandhi), Manmohini, Krishna, a friend.

Manmohini signs her autograph, Karachi Congress, 1931.

Women released from prison, Lahore, 1931.

Manmohini marries Amrit Lal Sahgal, 1935. Signing the register.

Sahgal Family, 1948. From left: Pradip, Manmohini, Saloni, Amrit, Anjali.

Manmohini runs for Congress, 1952. Jawaharlal Nehru is speaking.

Manmohini with Radhakrishnan, President of India, at the inauguration of Indian Council Social Welfare, 1961.

Manmohini Sahgal, New Delhi, 1970. At her desk at the Rashika Restaurant.

6

I Am Arrested, 1930

Early in October 1930, the special magistrate trying the Lahore Conspiracy Case pronounced his judgment. Bhagat Singh, Raj Guru, and Sukhdev were sentenced to death; the other conspirators were sentenced to prison for periods ranging from three to twenty years. Shyama and I attended the conspiracy case trial every day. Public sympathy was with these young men, and Bhagat Singh was our hero.

On the evening of October 7, 1930, the day the judgment was pronounced, an urgent meeting was called to condemn the harsh sentences. Public resentment was great, and a large crowd showed up in spite of the short notice given. The meeting was presided over by Mr. Jawan Lal Kapur, later a judge of the Supreme Court in independent India. All the top leaders of the Punjab Congress, including my mother, were in prison, so we had to arrange the meeting ourselves. The meeting was called by the Bhagat Singh Defense Committee and the Lahore District Congress Committee. After the usual speeches, it was unanimously decided to call for a *hartal* the next day. As president of the Lahore Student Union, I called on the students to absent themselves from classes. After a hurried consultation with my colleagues, it was decided that the student union would picket Government College for Men and Forman Christian College, the two most prestigious educational institutions in Lahore. In between these two colleges was the

Law College, so we decided to post pickets there as well.

I requested that Mr. Kapur send word to the women volunteers on the roster of the District Congress Committee, asking them to assemble at the district office early the next morning. Mr. Kapur thought it would be a good idea if I went over to his house on Begum Road the next morning so that we could plan our movements for the day. The meeting then dispersed.

When I left home on the morning of October 8, 1930, I had a strong feeling that I would not be returning home that day. My elder sister Janak left for college as usual. She was a lecturer in English at Lahore College for Women, a government institution. I sent my younger sister Shyama to get our friend Swadesh Kumari from her house, go to the district office, collect all the women assembled there, and post them at the three colleges. I would join her at Government College for Men as soon as I was free. When I got to Mr. Kapur's residence, he informed me that the District Congress Committee felt that the *hartal*, to be effective, needed more organizing. One night's notice was not sufficient, so the committee decided to call for a *hartal* on October 9. I replied that since the student union had announced a *hartal* for October 8, we would go ahead with our program and the Congress could organize the general strike for the next day.

I asked Mr. Kapur to go to the District Congress Office and ask six male volunteers to meet me as soon as possible at Government College, New Hostel Gate. I then proceeded to Government College to find that Shyama and Swadesh had already posted women volunteers at Forman Christian College, the Law College, and Government College.

Picketing was in full swing and the roads were swarming with people. The student community is the same the world over. Any excitement is enough to keep them away from their lectures, and here was excitement with a vengeance. Never in the history of any university in India had educational institutions been picketed by a group of young women while the male students stood by to cheer them. When I got to the Government College, I found that I was the "odd man out," so to say, so I spent my time going from one gate of the college to the other, trying to keep the roads clear for traffic. On the side road was the entrance to the District Courts, but the boundary wall was crowded with people. I do not think any work was done in court that morning.

My principal, Mr. H.L.O. Garrett, had just returned from a long leave of absence. He had been rejoicing that the troublesome Miss Zutshi was no longer in college, when word was sent to his residence that she had returned to create even more trouble by picketing the college. Mr. Garrett left whatever he was doing and rushed to the college. When he saw me standing there he remarked, "So, you are back!" I am told that he then telephoned the police and asked them to take away Miss Zutshi, who was making a nuisance of herself. In their rush to get there, the police could not lay their hands on an official transport, so they commandeered a car to drive them to Government College. The male volunteers had just arrived, and I had left the gate to post them at strategic points. The police did not recognize me and were never known to be very intelligent in making inquiries. They had been told to arrest Miss Zutshi, who was standing at the gate opposite the new hostel. They found two young women there, and, presuming one of them to be me, promptly arrested them both. When I heard of their arrest, I went and stood alone at the gate, challenging the students to enter the college if they dared. As the day wore on, the excitement and enthusiasm became more intense. The roads all around the college were packed with students. I was inundated by requests to come and organize picketing at a number of other colleges. I replied that I was already so involved with one college that I had no time to go elsewhere. I urged the students to organize picketing in their own colleges. But this was quite unnecessary. With so many students absent, it was unlikely that classes were held in their colleges.

Meanwhile, the principal was getting annoyed. Where were the police? The reply came that Miss Zutshi had already been arrested and was on her way to prison. The principal was dancing mad. Miss Zutshi was still at the gate, he roared at the police authorities. Who had they arrested? They had no idea. Presuming that Miss Zutshi was a dangerous person, they were taking no risks. This time they sent a prison van with a large posse of police to arrest me. To cover up their mistake, they decided to arrest everyone picketing the colleges. So the young women from Forman Christian College and the Law College were rounded up. But the real excitement and the real challenge was at Government College. I was arrested. Meanwhile, Shyama and Swadesh were warned by friends to be ready, as their turn would be coming soon.

All Congress workers had been instructed by the local High Command not to carry any valuables (money, jewelry, even fountain pens) in their purses or bags, as they could be confiscated by the police in lieu of fines that would be imposed. Raj Rani, one of the two girls mistakenly arrested at the gate, was wearing a gold necklace and gold bangles. She left these with me. I had some cash and my fountain pen, which, with the gold jewelry, added up to a tidy sum. When the police came for me with the prison van, the crowd increased tenfold and became very resistant. They did not like the idea of a young woman being taken away in a prison van so the police were anxious to do their duty and hurry away. But I would not leave until I had handed over my purse to someone I knew well. Meanwhile, I refused to budge. Finally, one of my colleagues from the student union, Lajpat Rai, came, and I handed him the purse. I then allowed myself to be arrested and boarded the police van. The prison van was an oblong steel structure on wheels with two very narrow benches (only about six inches wide) attached to each side, running the length of the van. The door, also made of steel, was padlocked from the outside. The only air came from a four-inch-wide steel network opening, which extended along the walls just above the benches. On the driver's side were two steel network partitions that enabled the police to keep an eye on the prisoners inside. I had the honor of being the first woman to be arrested and to travel in this van. Soon after my arrest, Shyama and Swadesh were also arrested. When there were no more women, the young men took over the picketing. The Law College closed early, so no attention was paid to it. Forman Christian College did not merit any attention either. The principal there had refrained from calling in the police, so all the resentment of the young men was concentrated on Government College. The authorities at Government College escalated tension by calling in the police; otherwise, this might have been a peaceful demonstration. After all, if there were no classes for one day, no one would lose very much, but to call in the police just to have one young woman removed angered the student community.

The police had to come again and again in their effort to put a stop to this. Tempers ran high on both sides. Finally the police had to resort to a *lathi*-charge to disperse the crowd. By 2:30 P.M., sixteen women and thirty-five men, mostly college students, had been arrested. Never had Lahore witnessed so many arrests in one day.

Soon after my arrest, Lajpat Rai telephoned Janak at her college to relay the news and to tell her that Shyama would soon follow. Janak asked her principal, Miss Harrison, for leave for the rest of the day, explaining what had happened and the fact that Mother was already in prison. She would have to make the arrangements to send our clothes and food to the jail and inform Father, in Allahabad, about what had happened. Miss Harrison curtly refused her request. Janak was so upset that she promptly wrote out her resignation from the college, handed it to her principal, and walked out. She came home and packed a few things for me, Shyama, and herself as well, because she had now decided to court arrest. She then wrote a telegram for Father, left it with the servants with instructions to send it if she did not return home by 4:00 P.M., and left the house. Janak reached Government College just as Shyama and Swadesh were being taken away. She announced to the assembled crowd that since her two younger sisters had been arrested she had come to court arrest. The authorities were in no mood to discriminate as to who had been involved in the actual picketing and who had not. Before she knew what was happening, she was whisked away in a car and driven straight to the office of the district magistrate, Mr. Edgar Lewis. Unknown to her, I was sitting in the prison van waiting for the arrest warrants to be signed. Shyama and Swadesh had already been taken inside the office to have their formalities completed. I was deemed to be too dangerous to be allowed to leave the van, even with a police guard. After the formalities were over, Shyama and Swadesh joined me in the van, but for some reason it did not move. I supposed that the police were waiting to see how many more women would be arrested, and we were surprised when the door was unlocked and in stepped Janak. Having had a glimpse of a posh car out on the road, we presumed that she had come to see us, but she calmly informed us that she had resigned her job and had also been arrested. And so we were all brought to the female jail.

While waiting in the prison van I began worrying about what was happening at Government College. I felt responsible for organizing the picketing and began to worry that some untoward incident might happen. My main concern was contacting Mr. Jawan Lal Kapur. I could not leave the van to telephone him. After scanning the crowd for many anxious moments, I saw a lone bicyclist. I shouted to him to stop and asked him to carry a message to Mr. Jawan Lal Kapur at 3 Begum Road. He was to tell Mr. Kapur that all the young women picketing Government College had been arrested and that he needed to go immediately to the college. The intensity of public sympathy could be gauged by the fact that although this young man could not see me, he could hear a woman's voice from a stationary prison van and guessed what had happened. He listened to my plea and delivered the message. Later, Mr. Kapur told me that a young man had come to bring the news of the wholesale arrest of women at Government College.

After Janak's arrest, Lajpat Rai called *Anand Bhavan* at Allahabad and informed Mrs. Kamla Nehru of our arrest. He was not able to contact my father directly as we had no telephone. Mrs. Nehru went over to our house, smilingly congratulated my father, and gave him the message. Pandit Motilal and Jawaharlal were already in prison. On learning of our arrest, Motilal remarked that he was very happy that three generations of his family were then in jail. The Uttar Pradesh government was not resorting to such harsh measures at that time. It was not until January 1931 that the Uttar Pradesh authorities made their first arrest of women, beginning with Mrs. Kamla Nehru. After that, others were arrested: Mrs. Vijayalakshmi Pandit, her sister Krishna, and Mrs. Uma Nehru.

We were excited and enthusiastic about being taken to prison. We felt as if a great honor had been conferred on us. We shouted slogans and sang national songs while waiting for the formalities to be completed. In fact, the three of us, my sisters and I, dearly hoped to be imprisoned three times so we would be termed "habitual offenders."

Word had already reached Mother and the other women inside the prison that a fresh batch of young women had been arrested and that Shyama and I were among them. Each new entrant, whether people knew her or not, was cheered by those already in prison. Not only did it add spice to the otherwise dull and monotonous existence in prison; it was evidence for us that the *satyagraha* movement was alive and confirmation that our sacrifices had not been made in vain. When we arrived, the women were gathered near the big black iron gate, trying to see the new arrivals. Mother was worried that poor Janak would be left all alone in the house.

Meanwhile, we were outside the prison office waiting to be processed. The prison office was a small, unimpressive building just outside the main prison. In front of it was a huge iron gate with bars and at the back a huge black sheet of solid iron serving as another gate. This rectangular building housed the jailor's office, another small room adjacent to it, and the store rooms for uniforms and supplies. A narrow verandah served as the visitors' room. A warden sat just inside the front gate acting as a sort of timekeeper. His duty was to sound the passing of every hour and half-hour on a gong.

As we sang songs and shouted slogans, our voices echoed and reechoed in the narrow confines of the office block. The poor jailor, Bakshi Suggarmal, was so distracted that he rushed out of his office and implored us to be quiet so that he could take us into custody. The police were anxious to be off. Until then, Bakshi Suggarmal had led a very peaceful life. Mother had been arrested in August, Pooran Devi in September, and only a few other women from Delhi and other places. Suddenly, he had to take charge of sixteen women, most of whom were young and out to create trouble for the authorities. What he did not know at that time was that a little later he would have to take charge of four small children. One of our friends, Shakuntala Chawla, had left three small children behind and another friend one child. Once they heard of their wives' arrest, the husbands brought these children to be with their mothers.

At last the formalities were complete and we were ushered into the jail. What celebrations there were then! We were treated as heroines coming home. Everyone rejoiced that there had been so many arrests in one day, although we did not yet know that thirty-five young men had been arrested. That sixteen women had been arrested from sleepy Lahore was a great thing! The movement would certainly continue. Since the magistrate had forgotten to classify us in A, B, or C categories, we all stayed together. The jail authorities immediately provided us with dry rations because it would be evening before we could get food from our respective homes. This became a picnic lunch, with everyone helping with the cooking and talking excitedly. The trial magistrate, Mr. C.H. Disney, came in the afternoon and informed us that our trial would begin the next morning on the jail premises. He classified us as A and B prisoners and left. Whether he left instructions with the jailor or the latter thought of it himself, I do not know, but soon after he left, the jailor said he was separating A and B prisoners. B prisoners were to be taken to another barracks in a separate compound where they would be locked up at night. We did not personally know all the women who had come with us, and we were afraid that a few of them might be persuaded to apologize in court the next day and be released. That would be a great setback to the movement. We protested that this classification should take effect after the trial was over. Until then, we were all pretrial prisoners entitled to the same privileges, that is, wearing our own clothes and receiving food from home. The jailor was adamant. He said he had to obey the orders of the magistrate. We were equally determined to demand our rights. The jailor tried persuasion first and then threatened to have the B group forcibly removed. He left us, saying that he would round up his wardresses who would not hesitate to drag the B group off. At that time, we had no idea of the geography of the prison. We later on discovered that the class B barracks was in a separate compound, part of a much larger compound that housed other buildings used for class C prisoners and long-term prisoners. It also housed the hospital block and solitary cells. It was quite a distance from our barracks. Had the jailor carried out his threat we would have been badly hurt, but we squatted in a circle, with our arms linked, on the hard earthen floor outside the A barracks, determined to resist all efforts to break up our group. Mother threatened to deal with the wardresses should they so much as lay a finger on any of her daughters.

We sat like this until it became pitch dark. The jail compound was quiet and peaceful. No sinister figures came out of the office. Some friends had sent us dinner, but we returned it as we were in no mood to eat. The other women were so upset at these developments that they had not cooked for themselves either. Finally, at about 9:00 P.M., Satyavati* went to the office and asked the jailor what he intended to do, as the women were still squatting. Was he going to carry out his threat of dragging them off? Was he prepared to face public censure if any of the women were manhandled and hurt? He laughed and said to tell the women not to be silly but to go to bed as it was quite late. As we had eaten no dinner we went to sleep hungry, but we were triumphant after our long and eventful day.

The next morning the magistrate, hearing of our defiance, decided to hold our trial in two groups. Those arrested from Government College would form one group and the other group would consist of women arrested from Forman Christian College and the Law College. We protested that this made no sense, because the offense was the same. But the magistrate, egged on by the police, would not listen. We refused to leave the class A barracks and sent word through the jailor that the trial could be held in absentia because we were not putting up

---

* Satyavati was the granddaughter of Swami Shraddhanand, the leader of the Furukula section of the *Arya Samaj* [a Hindu reformist society]. Known as a great educator and fearless leader, Shraddhanand joined the political movement in 1919.

any defense. After the so-called trial, the magistrate could let us know what sentence had been passed. I must confess that the magistrate, Mr. Disney, was a nice and friendly person. He had conducted Mother's trial and felt he knew the family. He finally acceded to our request, and all of us were brought in together. To our dismay, we found that "court" was being held in the narrow verandah adjacent to the jailor's office. There was hardly any room for us, the police, and the witnesses. Our relatives and friends, who had come in large numbers, had been left standing in the sun. We again protested and demanded that all our relatives and friends be present at the trial since that was allowed according to the *Jail Manual*. The magistrate agreed, but permitted only two relatives per prisoner. Our demand was for five per head, since Swadesh had three younger sisters as well as her parents. The magistrate, wedded to his sense of magisterial dignity, would not agree and thus created an impasse. He tried to reason with us that lack of space prevented him from from honoring our request. But we three sisters had been to Mother's trial. It was held in the hospital compound in a very big hall. Mother had been alone and did not need all that space. We were so many; why could we not use that hall again? The magistrate, left to himself, might have agreed, but the public prosecutor, an Indian police officer, said something to him that made him take a firm stand. He ordered that irrespective of what the prisoners felt or said, the trial would go on. Not ready to be silenced by him, we started singing national songs. Hearing the refrain, our friends inside the jail and the huge crowd outside joined in with gusto. Can you imagine the din it created in that narrow space! The magistrate looked on helplessly. The noise was so great that nothing could be heard. In desperation he postponed the trial to the next day and asked the jailor to send us back to our barracks.

The crowd dispersed and came back in even larger numbers the next day. Meanwhile, Father had arrived from Allahabad. The next morning when he visited us in prison, the magistrate complained to him about the unruly behavior of his daughters. The magistrate described us as the ringleaders. Father pacified him and came to see us. We told him of our demand of five relatives each and why we had chosen that number. The court could easily assemble in the prison hospital barracks. Not only did it have a large hall but a big compound as well. He also knew of it, as Mother's trial had been held there. Father assured us that everything would be done according to our wishes. He persuaded the magistrate to agree to a different venue and took on the responsibility of inquiring who the prisoners' relatives were. He maneuvered it in such a manner that all those five hundred or more people gathered outside the jail were comfortably accommodated on the floor on dhurries. And so the trial began. It was a short affair, and since it was our first offense we were sentenced to only one month's simple imprisonment and a fine of fifty rupees. If we refused to pay the fine we would be jailed for another fifteen days.

And so we settled down to our life in prison. Those who were class B prisoners were accommodated in a huge barracks where everyone slept on the floor. They were not permitted to leave their compound, the gates of which were locked at night. All of us, whether class A or B, were given dry rations and one uncooked vegetable. Class A and B prisoners could have food sent from home. Cooking utensils were provided by the jail authorities. Class B prisoners had to cook and do other domestic chores themselves, whereas one "helper" was provided for every four class A prisoners. Usually they clubbed together in groups of three or four and divided the work among themselves. The class C prisoners got cooked food from the jail kitchen and had to wear regulation prison uniforms. There were also differences in the number of visits allowed and the number of letters that could be sent and received. This classification was based on the prisoner's status before entering jail, but it did not apply to revolutionaries, who were declared "delinquents" by the the government and therefore excluded from this classification. As class A prisoners we were free to visit our class B and C friends, though they could not leave their compounds. This coming and going kept us all occupied.

We used to hold tea parties in the class B barracks, getting snacks from outside whenever someone's relative came to visit. Some Indian sweets are very spongy and sweet, and some, particularly *raj bhoj*, are very large. If anyone wanted to send a message to all of us it was slipped inside a *raj bhoj*. We always enjoyed these tea parties, particularly if there was a secret message for all of us.

Mother was the undisputed leader of all the political prisoners. Lahore Jail was the only jail for women in the region, which included the Northwest Frontier Province, Delhi, and the entire Punjab. There were a number of women there from Lyallpur and Amritsar, most of them in class C barracks. Mother was kept busy mediating the petty quarrels that arose among the prisoners and dealing with the prison authorities.

Women were prepared to sacrifice a great deal for the country. One woman had been arrested with us and placed in class C barracks. Her husband, a petty shopkeeper in the walled city, had already left for work when his wife was informed that she would be needed at the District Congress office that morning. It never occurred to her to disregard the summons, although she had not anticipated being arrested. So she came along, joined the demonstration, and was arrested. Her husband, when he came to know of all this, was incensed. He did not come to the trial and openly showed his displeasure. He even sent a message to his wife that after her release she could not return home. The poor woman was greatly upset. When Mother heard about this, she sent some Congress workers to see him and explain to him what a great honor it was for him and other members of his family to have his wife in prison. He replied that he was well aware of the honor and was very proud of his wife, but he was expressing his displeasure because she had left the house without his permission. Had he been asked he would have been only too happy to let her go. After all, it was with his permission that she had had her name registered on the roster of volunteers at the District Congress office and it was with his full concurrence that she attended all Congress meetings and processions. When the circumstances were explained to him, the misunderstanding was cleared up. I still remember how upset this poor woman was. She could easily have tendered an apology to the authorities, gone home, and placated her husband, but she stuck with her political duty in spite of her husband's threats.

Those of us who were class A prisoners lived in an old barracks consisting of four very small rooms (eight square feet) with attached baths and a fairly narrow verandah. On all sides there were thick iron bars. This was the old European ward. It housed my mother, my sisters, and me; Mrs. Asaf Ali; Mrs. Rajpati Kaul (Kamla Nehru's mother); Satyavati, her sister Kaushalya, her mother Srimati Ved Kumar (Swami Shraddhanand's daughter), and her aunt, Mrs. Indra; Mrs. Mahavir Tyaji; Parvati Devi (Lala Lajpat Rai's daughter); Chand Kohli; Chando Bibi; Parvati Devi from Delhi; Khurshed Naoroji (Dadabhai Naoroji's granddaughter); Sushila Mohan; and a few others. The rooms being small, no one could sleep on beds, though we were permitted the use of them. The mattresses given to us were filled with straw instead of cotton wool and were bumpy and most uncomfortable. They served as beds at night and during the day we rolled them up and placed them together to form a kind of divan to sit on, Indian fashion. One room served as a bedroom, sitting room, and dining room for Mother, my sisters, and me and Aruna Asaf Ali. Later we were joined by Sushila Mohan. Each of us was given a small six-inch-square stool; there were no tables. The senior ladies—Mother, Mrs. Kaul, and Srimati Ved Kumari—slept on the verandah on *charpoys* [string-woven cots] that were so high that getting on and off them was really a problem.

The normal rule in the prison was for all prisoners to line up with their kits neatly rolled and utensils clean and shiny whenever the superintendent came around for his weekly inspection. We had decided from the first day that since we were not criminals we would not observe this rule. One representative from each category of political prisoner would meet the superintendent at the door of the barracks, explain her group's demands, and answer any questions. The rest of us would remain indoors and continue with whatever we were doing. In short, the rounds of the superintendent would have no special significance for us. The superintendent, Colonel P.D. Chopra, although he was an Indian, resented our behavior and took it as an affront to his prestige. He sent word to Mother that if her three daughters would not behave and toe the line, he would have us transferred to the Gujarat Jail if we were arrested again in northern India. Mother replied that, had chairs been provided, the political prisoners would meet his request. But it was difficult and undignified to jump down from unusually high *charpoys*, nor would we agree to line up as the ordinary criminals were expected to do. From the class A group it was only Mother who met him at the barracks door.

Our days were spent trying to do what we had little leisure to do outside. Many of the women were busy housewives with little children and homes to look after. Those who knew a little English tried to brush up on it. Shyama and I decided to learn Urdu with Mother as our teacher. She was always so busy that she had little time to teach, but we did get books from the proprietor of Paisa Akhbar, a local bookstore. After lunch, the time for our lesson, Mother would go to sleep, and so we made little progress. Most of us spent our time embroidering saris. A young cousin posted in Agra used to keep us well supplied with fiction and magazines. Other books were smuggled in. I remember reading V.D. Savarkar's *Indian War of Independence of 1857* in jail.

We used to show some of these books to the jailor to show that they were harmless. Any suspicious books he kept overnight to show to the superintendent for his approval. He had a particular aversion to any book title that had the letters "tion" in it, deducing that "tion" stood for "revolution." He was not prepared to permit us to read such books. I received a book with "education" in the title, and when I asked his permission to take it to my room, it was denied me. In vain I argued that it had nothing to do with revolution but he was adamant. He kept pointing to the four letters "tion," insisting that it was seditious. Finally, I gave up and left the book on his desk to be scrutinized by the superintendent. I got the book the next day; the poor jailor looked very sheepish when he delivered it. Such incidents kept us amused and gave us food for gossip.

Among us was a lady by the name of Rup Kaur whose eldest son, Sampuran Singh Tandon, was a minor revolutionary. When he came to visit his mother in prison, he said he wanted to meet the young woman who had created so much excitement in Lahore. The rules for visiting were not strictly applied, so when Rup Kaur asked the jailor, I was sent for. I do not know what sort of a person Sampuran Singh expected to see, but he seemed very surprised to see a harmless-looking young woman like myself. When I was released from prison, he came to see me with a message from his leaders asking me to join the revolutionary movement. I thanked him for the honor but said that I did not want to live in hiding, doubting all neighbors and friends, and expecting to be arrested at any time.

It was at this time that I had to go to Gujarat (in the Punjab) to appear as a defense witness in a case against Sardool Singh, a Vice-President, and Ladha Ram, the General Secretary, of the student union.

At the beginning of the *satyagraha* movement (May 1930), these two had been sent to organize a student union in Gujrat, a small city in the western Punjab located about sixty miles from Lahore. They were immediately arrested on two counts: seditious speeches and *dacoity*.* They did not contest the first charge, but as respectable citizens denied the second. Both were released on bail. As I was the President of the student union, they had cited me as a defense witness. When I was called as witness I was in prison myself, so the police came to the Lahore Female Jail with the summons. The jailor sent for Mother and explained the case. She was very worried about her daughter traveling to Gujrat in police custody, but she realized that the summons could not be ignored. So she asked the jailor if one of the wardresses could

---

*Robbery by a gang of five or more.

accompany me as an escort. The superintendent must have been in a good mood that day, for he agreed immediately. I left the prison accompanied by Rukmini, the wardress, and the police. Although our sentence was only for six weeks, we were all hankering for a glimpse of the outside world. My sisters and other young friends envied me this trip.

The Delhi group had been regaling us with stories about how they had persuaded their police escorts to let them travel second-class by train when they were being brought to Lahore. Without mentioning it to anyone, I decided I would travel second-class to Gujrat. The prison van took me to the railway police headquarters. While the subinspector-in-charge went inside, I was left locked in the van. I saw that time was running out, and I had not yet voiced my request for traveling second-class. I knocked loudly on the door of the van. As soon as it was opened I said, "Please go and tell your officer that I want to travel second-class." The door was banged shut in my face, but my message was conveyed to the young subinspector. He came and said that if I paid the difference in fares, for myself and my police escort, I could certainly travel second-class. I replied that I had no money, and, even if I had, I would not pay since I was not going to Gujrat of my own accord. Once again the door was shut abruptly. I knocked again. When the door opened, I made it clear that I was very serious and that no power on earth could make me travel third-class. An argument started. The police said that since I was in their custody, I would have to do as I was told. To that I replied that I would not get out of the van at the station. They would have to drag me out and if they were prepared for that scene and any incident that might result, then they could proceed as they wished. But they should also remember that Lahore was a busy station. How would they handle it if a crowd collected to see one lone young woman offering *satyagraha*?

The subinspector went to consult somebody. Since the distance between Lahore and Gujrat was not great, they agreed to sanction the second-class fare for me and for my escort. In the midst of all of this, the Gujrat Mail left, so we had to leave by a passenger train leaving Lahore at 6:00 P.M. Once again the authorities made a tactical blunder. I had to travel in a second-class compartment, the outside of which carried the word "Prisoner" written in bold letters. I was guarded by two constables fully armed with rifles and bayonets. When I got into the compartment with my friend the subinspector, I noticed Rukmini standing outside on the platform. On my inquiring as to why she was not coming in, I was told that she had a third-class pass given to her by the prison authorities and would travel in a separate compartment. I hurriedly got out of the train and told the subinspector that I would not go if Rukmini could not sit in the same compartment with me. Again the arguments started. Finally, seeing that the train was about to start, the subinspector reluctantly agreed to pay extra for Rukmini, and we finally left for Gujrat. On the way, this police officer, a friendly young Muslim, explained that he had to carry out his orders and was not personally responsible for any inconvenience I suffered. I told him that I understood all that and did not blame him for anything. He offered me an Urdu book to read on the long journey, but unfortunately I did not know the language.

We arrived at our destination at 10:00 P.M. In the dim light of the station platform I found one inspector and four constables, all armed to the teeth, waiting to receive me. I was then escorted to the subjail.

Hearing of the arrival of a young woman, local Congress workers in prison had already gotten the superintendent's permission to provide breakfast and lunch for me from their homes. All the top Congress leaders of the Punjab and Delhi were in the Gujrat Special Jail. Maulana Abdul Kalam Azad, whom I had known since my childhood, Asaf Ali, Deshbandhu Gupta, and Dr. Gopi Chand, among others, had all requested that I stay with them. The superintendent would not agree. How could he permit a young woman to spend any time in a men's prison? In vain Maulana Azad and others protested that I was like a daughter to them and that they would be happy to look after me. But he would not listen. The subjail had a wardress, so I was lodged there.

After breakfast the next morning, I was taken to court in an open bus escorted by one inspector, one subinspector, and six fully armed constables. It created a sensation in sleepy Gujrat. After the evidence was concluded, I was brought back to the subjail for lunch, and then we left for the station to catch the mail to Lahore. Since no separate compartment could be made available for me at such short notice, the subinspector apologetically said I would have to travel in a men's compartment as I was in his custody. I could not travel in a women's compartment with only the jail wardress as an escort. But I was admonished not to talk to any of the passengers. No one said anything, but they must have been greatly intrigued as to who I was.

We reached Lahore and I was taken to the police office at the railway station to have dinner. I protested that it was much too early to eat and I would prefer having my meal with my family in prison. But I was told that there was a police regulation that I must be fed before being dropped home. Mother was already getting restive and had inquired when I would be returning. She heaved a sigh of relief when I returned safe and sound after an exciting two-day visit to Gujrat.

We were actually sorry when our six weeks were over. It was great fun to be in prison, and we had become accustomed to life within those four walls. With so many women from different parts of the country, we were kept busy and life was interesting. Each new arrival was greeted with shouted slogans and nationalist songs.

It was customary that prisoners be informed of the date and time of their release so they could inform their relations. As the day of our release drew near, we asked the jailor when we would be released. He gave the date as November 22, 1930, and the time as 8:00 A.M. We passed this time and date on to our relatives and friends. November 21 was to be our last night in prison and we planned to celebrate in a big way! Imagine our consternation when the jailor suddenly appeared at 8:00 P.M. on the twenty-first and informed us that our release warrants had arrived and that we were to leave immediately. No one had even had her dinner. In fact, we were still busy cooking. We protested. Where were we to go on a cold winter night? Our relatives were expected in the morning. Swadesh's parents had moved to another locality. But the jailor said he was powerless. He had received his orders from the government in the form of those release warrants. He could not keep us in prison for an hour after that. He went to the class B barracks, kicked the food off the fire, threw the prisoners' belongings out, and locked the cells. We knew we had no option so we hurriedly packed and left our cells.

For the sixteen of us and the four children, along with boxes and bedrolls, we could find only five *tongas*. The jail was outside the city, and every one of us lived in a different locality. How were we to get home with only five *tongas* at our disposal? Some of the women had never been out so late at night unescorted by their menfolk. Would the authorities provide us with more *tongas*? The jailor said no; the five *tongas* they had arranged were adequate and could take us all by turns. We pointed out to him that this exercise could perhaps take the entire night, but he would not relent. He mentioned that no more *tongas* were available in the city of Lahore, and he expected us to believe that! In vain we pointed out the clause in the *Jail Manual* that said each prisoner was entitled to one *tonga* at the time of release. But who was there to listen? The jail authorities had said that no more *tongas* were to be had, and they had to stick to it. We had no option but to offer *satyagraha* in the true Gandhian style. We decided to spend the night squatting outside the jail gates until our relatives came to fetch us or adequate transport was provided.

We started to make ourselves as comfortable as possible, although it was bitter cold. We made a sort of a platform with our trunks joined together outside the jail gates and spread our bedding over them. The jailor, seeing our intent, hurriedly telephoned his colleague, the jailor of the Borstal Jail, who was a bearded Muslim. He came and in a fatherly way patted me on the head and offered his personal *tonga* to take us three sisters home. We repeated our demand for more *tongas*, but once a particular stand was taken by our jailor, the Borstal jailor had to support him. So he went away disappointed. Meanwhile, seeing that the situation was getting out of hand, the jailor telephoned the superintendent, who came over at once, accompanied by the Deputy Inspector General of Prisons, Colonel N.D. Puri, an Indian and a friend of the family. They offered my two sisters and me their cars if we would consent to leave the others stranded and go home. On our repeating our demand for adequate transport for all of us, they were equally adamant in not conceding, so we informed them that we had no other alternative but to offer *satyagraha*. We were not going home and leaving our friends in the lurch.

Mother and the other women, hearing of our dispute, wanted to come out and talk to the jailor, but he was not talking to anybody. He had announced his decision that no more *tongas* were available in Lahore and that was that. The *tongas* were dismissed, but the drivers had witnessed all this rumpus and naturally their sympathies were all for us. Besides taking into consideration the location of the female jail, miles away from all habitation, even from Borstal Jail, surrounded on all sides by large trees that threw their dark shadows everywhere, and acres of fields all round, it was certainly a sinister and forbidding place. Anything could happen to a batch of rebellious young women like ourselves who were making things uncomfortable for the authorities. So the *tonga* drivers decided to stay on to protect us against untoward incidents. If the jail authorities had so desired, they could have had us beaten up or otherwise molested. Then, who would be there to listen to our cries for help? But with the supreme confidence of youth, we told them that we were quite safe and they could go home. If they wanted to help us, they could carry a note to our eldest sister, Chandra, who had come from Calcutta to keep the house open for us and attend to all our wants. Also, we wanted one *tongawalla* [*tonga* driver] to carry a note to the press of our early release. They agreed. Chandra was so alarmed at the news that she hurriedly came to the jail, though it was long past midnight. She remonstrated with us for our foolhardiness. If we fell seriously ill with pneumonia, the British government would not be sorry. But the question of transport had become a matter of prestige for us, and we were not going to give in even if we fell sick later on. Chandra went home worried and upset. She dispatched a telegram to Father reading, "Sisters released but spending night in open outside jail." Not being on the spot and not knowing the circumstances, he and the family in Allahabad were very worried.

I think that it was the longest night I have ever spent. At first, we sang national songs, but gradually our enthusiasm for singing wore off. We were sleepy, cold, and uncomfortable and wanted the night to be over soon. The warden timekeeper was sitting just inside the gate, and every now and again we would say to him, "Baba, please sound the gong! Surely the hour has passed!" He would reply very philosophically, "The night will take its time in passing. Sounding the gong every fifteen minutes would not bring the dawn soon." How true. The weary night finally passed and dawn was about to break. Tired of sitting, we wandered off to the nearest tap and started our morning ablutions.

Chandra could hardly sleep for worry nor could she sit at home, so the moment it was light enough to see, she had a large urn of tea prepared and came over to the jail. She was surprised to see us wandering about quite casually. But a hot cup of tea was very welcome after a cold and uncomfortable night. Mother had spent the entire night sitting on the floor of the cell. She refused to lie down since her daughters were forced to sit up all night outside the jail gate in the bitter cold.

In the morning, the class A prisoners pooled their rations of sugar, tea, and milk and sent us a large urn of tea with a small plate of fried almonds. It was all they had with them. None of us had had our dinner the previous night, and we were very hungry. The jailor permitted tea to be served to us but refused the plate of almonds, saying that no food from prison could be given to discharged prisoners. Mother sent a message to the jailor through the warden that almonds were not part of the jail ration and the prisoners could do as they wished with them. But the jailor refused to listen. He had the plate returned to Mother and the other ladies standing just behind the massive iron gate leading to the jail premises. They would not accept it, so a major tussle between the class A ladies and the jailor ensued. Exasperated, Mother shouted, "Let Bakshiji [the jailor] eat it himself, we are not going to take it back." It was only then that this small plate of almonds was given to us.

The *tongawalla* who had visited the press representative at 2:00 A.M. had evidently done his job well. The morning papers, both in English and in the vernacular, carried news of our dramatic release and subsequent *satyagraha* outside the jail. The story was in bold letters as "stop press news." Had we been released in the morning at the appointed time, only a handful of people, mostly relatives, would have come to the jail to receive us, and there would have been no crowd or demonstration. As it was, everybody came rushing to the jail to see what was happening and whether we were all safe. Resentment ran high. We had been the first batch of women to be imprisoned and so had brought honor to their town, and we were the first batch to be released. How dare the authorities treat us so shabbily! Soon a mammoth crowd collected outside the jail. The demonstration the government wanted to avoid was now happening. The people insisted on taking us out in a procession which would terminate at our house on Panj Mahal Road.

When we arrived home it was decided that we would have a community lunch for everyone. Some rushed to the market for purchases, the women lighted fires and started cooking, and our lawn looked like it was the site of a *mela* [fair]. By 4:00 P.M. everyone had eaten and the crowd had dispersed. The public meeting to welcome us back was organized by the District Congress Committee for the next day.

We soon settled down to a life of meetings and processions and fortnightly visits with Mother. But we felt that this life would not last long. We were looking for opportunities that would land us in prison again.

7

Fighting the Raj

The convocation of the University of Punjab was considered a grand occasion and was scheduled for soon after my release from prison. Not content with having had me arrested, my principal, Mr. Garrett, asked the Senate (the governing body of the university) to withhold my master's degree. We had been hearing rumors to this effect while I was still in prison. Mother knew that she was powerless behind bars, but she encouraged the people of Lahore to take steps to prevent this injustice to her daughter. I had passed the examination through my own efforts, so why should I be deprived of the degree? Whether they were responding to public pressure or their own good sense, the members of the Senate threw out this resolution. I remember I purchased a new sari for this occasion. Receiving a degree is an important time in any student's life, but for me it was doubly so because I had nearly lost the right to write the letters M.A. after my name.

Dr. S. Radhakrishnan, the Vice-Chancellor of Andhra University, had been asked to deliver the convocation address. Since I was the only woman in my class, I was taken up onto the dais to receive my degree from the hands of the Chancellor of the University and Governor of the Province, Sir Geoffrey De Montmorency. The hall echoed and reechoed with thunderous applause. Dr. Radhakrishnan was mystified since the same ovation was not awarded other women receiving academic distinctions. He inquired of the Governor how I had distinguished myself to be set apart so. He was informed that I had just been released from prison! This incident so impressed Dr. Radhakrishnan that he never forgot it. Later, when he came to Delhi as Vice-President and then as President of India, he used to tell the story frequently.

The convocation stands out in my mind for another reason. A revolutionary young man, Hari Kishan, had come all the way from the Northwest Frontier Province to shoot the Governor and had decided on this convocation as the best time to do so. I and some other students had met him earlier and knew of his plans. How he gained admission to the convocation ceremony will always remain a mystery. The convocation had concluded, the band had finished playing the British national anthem, and the Chancellor, accompanied by Dr. Radhakrishnan, had started walking toward the exit gate. He was followed by the Vice-Chancellor, Dr. A.C. Woolner, and the registrar, an Indian. These four men, two Englishmen and two Indians, walked toward Hari Kishan, who was keyed up and ready to shoot, but whose vision was blocked by the audience. Concerned with the safety of Dr. Radhakrishnan and the registrar, he aimed at the Governor—but his bullets missed their mark. The governor escaped unhurt, but a subinspector of police, Chanan Singh, was hit by a stray bullet and died. Another casualty was Dr. (Miss) Merchand of the Lady Hardinge Medical College, Delhi, who was sitting on the dais. After firing all the bullets, Hari Kishan threw away his revolver and stood quietly waiting to be arrested. I have never seen a more amazing sight. Immediately the hall was cleared of all the visitors, who ran with their chairs as shields over their heads. Pandemonium reigned. No one knew what had happened or what was about to happen. I was pushed onto the dais. When things calmed down, the police found Hari Kishan standing alone in an almost deserted hall. He was arrested and charged with murder. Although Subinspector Chanan Singh was killed by a stray bullet, the authorities maintained that his death was a deliberate murder, and Hari Kishan received the death sentence. The nationalists of Lahore felt they had lost a hero. Hari Kishan's name was added to the long list of young martyrs who had embraced death in the service of their motherland.

After sitting at home for a month or so after our release from prison, feeling terribly bored just attending public meetings, we three sisters decided the time had come to give another shock to the authorities in Lahore. One fine morning in January 1931, we got together with our friends Avinash, Shakuntala, and Shakuntala Chawla, sallied forth to the nearest market, and began to picket the shops. Everyone was taken by surprise. The Lahore District Congress Committee had not announced or arranged this event, but they appreciated any action that drew attention to the *satyagraha* movement. Even the police had an easy time of it. They had to respond to our action by arresting us which was exactly what we wanted. All six of us were rounded up and taken to the Lahore Female Jail, a place we had left barely six weeks earlier.

This time our trial magistrate was a certain Mr. Hassan Mahmud. He perhaps had orders to award us the maximum punishment to keep us out of mischief. At any rate, we were sentenced to one year's simple imprisonment. Profiting from our previous experience, we had made prior arrangements at home so that our eldest sister, Chandra, would not need to leave her home and come to Lahore to look after us.

We picked up life in prison where we had left off. The class A prisoners, including Mother, were all still there, as were many of our friends in classes B and C. But we were not destined to remain behind bars for long. The British Government had been given a jolt by the women of India. They had not expected our enthusiasm for courting arrest. We were not the meek, mild, illiterate Indian women, content to remain within the four walls of our homes, that they had made us out to be. I remember we had a young married woman with us in prison. She had lived in such seclusion that the mere sight of a red-turbaned police constable inspired fear in her, and yet here she was, cheerfully courting arrest. The Viceroy, Lord Irwin, invited Gandhiji for talks, and these talks led to the termination of the *satyagraha* movement. The Gandhi–Irwin Pact was signed on March 15, 1931. Political prisoners all over the country, except those imprisoned for violent acts, were immediately released.

Under this pact, certain concessions for salt were made, nonviolent picketing was permitted, the right to *satyagraha* for redress of agrarian grievances was conceded, and lands sold during the no-tax campaign were to be restored to their rightful owners. Congress agreed not to press for an inquiry into police excesses and undertook to see that two million rupees in unpaid taxes in Gujarat be paid. Lord Irwin left India three weeks after the pact was signed.

In Lahore there was a lot of confusion. Release warrants for the local prisoners were received, and we were released, but orders for many women from outside Lahore—Delhi, Amritsar, Lyall Pur,

Peshwar—had not yet come. Mother refused to go home while so many of her friends were still in prison. She asked the superintendent for permission to camp outside the jail until the women inside were freed. Colonel Sondhi, the superintendent, was the son of an old family friend and Congress leader from Jullundur, Raizada Hans Raj. Mindful of the bitter criticism his predecessor had to face when we spent the night squatting outside the jail, he readily agreed.

In no time a small camp city appeared outside the prison gates. It consisted of relatives of the women who were awaiting release, members of the public, and officeholders and volunteers of the Punjab Provincial Congress organization as well as the various District Congress Committees. We three sisters had ostensibly gone home, but we spent all our working hours in this camp. Mother was there day and night to boost the morale of those still behind bars. After three days, the release warrants finally arrived. What rejoicing there was!

At that time we considered the Gandhi–Irwin Pact a great moral victory for Congress. We did not realize that our pre-pact protests would have to be repeated within the year. Unfortunately, Gandhiji was no statesman. He was often swayed by sentiment and would sometimes overlook a golden opportunity. In fact, Gandhiji had had no good reason to call off the *satyagraha* movement; after all, the response from all over the country had been so overwhelming. Gandhi did not realize that the British, taken by surprise by the enthusiasm of the masses, only wanted time to tighten the government machinery for more repressive measures. This pact and the subsequent Round Table Conference in London were doomed to failure, as the British had no intention of parting with any power. While Gandhiji was in London, Jawaharlal was arrested in Uttar Pradesh and Abdul Ghaffar Khan in the Northwest Frontier Province. Ordinance rule* was established in Bengal. The government then tried to divide the *harijans* from the Hindus with the Communal Award of March 1932.† Upon his return to India, Gandhiji tried to meet with the new Viceroy, Lord Willingdon, but his request for an interview was refused. Congress had to revive

---

*Ordinance IX of 1931 gave extraordinary powers in terms of arrest and detention of anyone engaged in waging war against the King, inciting terrorism, or harboring absconders.
†The British Government gave separate seats in the legislature to different communities in each province. These were to be elected by separate electorates. Gandhi said he would fast to the death if this award were not extended to untouchables.

its program of noncooperation and civil disobedience.

After our release under the Gandhi–Irwin Pact, there was feverish activity among the younger Congress workers to press for the release of Bhagat Singh and his comrades, or at least to have their death sentences commuted to life terms. Gandhiji had not required the release of these young men in the terms of the pact, although he had pressed for it. When the Viceroy refused their release, Gandhi went ahead and signed. There was intense frustration and disappointment all over the country. Public meetings were held every day to impress upon the Viceroy that better relations would prevail between the Indian public and the British government if some leniency could be extended to the Lahore Conspiracy prisoners. But the Viceroy was adamant. He had achieved what he had been ordered to do, that is, break the back of the civil disobedience movement by offering a shallow peace. In any case, he was due to leave India in three weeks.

Chandra Shekhar Azad had asked Jawaharlal to interfere, but, ever loyal to Gandhiji, he did not. The government kept the date of the execution a secret, so the public kept a constant vigil in front of the Lahore Central Jail. Nevertheless, the execution came as a great surprise. I was at a public meeting late one evening when someone came and whispered a message to Dr. Mohammad Alam, who was presiding over the meeting. Without uttering a word, he got up and left the meeting with some other leaders. But bad news travels quickly, and soon everyone heard that Bhagat Singh, Raj Guru, and Sukhdev had been executed. Immediately, everyone rushed to the Central Jail. I went home first and informed Mother of the news, and together we went to the Central Jail.

It so happened that a local Congress leader, Pandit K. Santanam, lived very near the jail. At about 8:00 P.M. he had heard the inmates of the prison shouting "Bhagat Singh *Zindabad*" [Long live Bhagat Singh]. He guessed that something had happened and ran straight to the jail. There he met Bhagat Singh's father, Sardar Kishan Singh, and the members of his family, who had been hurriedly summoned to bid farewell to this brave son of India. The relatives of Raj Guru and Sukhdev were also there. All were in tears. The three young men had been hanged; their bodies cut into pieces, rolled in gunny bags, and taken to the banks of the river Sutlaj, opposite the city of Ferozepur. Here the bodies were consigned to flames, the pyres guarded by fully armed British soldiers. A villager saw the fire guarded by British soldiers from his cottage on the opposite bank and guessed what had happened. He immediately went to the house of the secretary of the District Congress Committee and relayed his suspicions. The secretary contacted Congress leaders in Lahore, and the fact that this was the secret site of the three young men's funeral pyres was confirmed. Immediately the place became a sacred pilgrimage ground.

The next morning, Bhagat Singh's sister, Amar Kaur, and some Congress leaders went to Ferozepur. The bodies could not be identified, even though the British soldiers had not bothered to light the pyre properly. Half-charred body pieces lay about. They were reverently gathered and brought to Lahore. There, three separate biers were set up with flowers and garlands, and the remains were taken in a huge procession to the river Ravi. On hearing the news, Gandhiji asked all Congress workers to form a silent procession as a sign of grief and protest. But the younger generation was so full of anger at this wanton behavior and desecration of their heroes that they were not prepared to listen to Gandhiji's advice. A separate procession was formed. I headed a procession of about six thousand students, but all the groups joined on the river Ravi, where homage was paid to the departed souls and the last rites were performed meticulously with respect and great affection. Jawaharlal wrote, "Bhagat Singh became a symbol, the act was forgotten, the symbol remained and within a few months, each town and village of the Punjab and to lesser extent in the rest of northern India has resounded with his name. Innumerable songs grew up around him and the popularity the man achieved was amazing."

Lord Irwin had been replaced as Viceroy by a staunch imperialist, and a reign of repression and terror soon began. For our part, we had learned not to fritter away our energies on impulsive actions. The first thing Mother did was strip the house bare of everything of value. Furnishings, carpets, crockery, clothes, silver, and jewelry were packed up and sent out. A minimum amount of money was left in the bank account, as the government took away all that they could lay their hands on.

One cunning scheme for securing an arrest was to post the ordinance order on the doors of well-known political workers. This order forbade people to join processions or meet with groups of more than five. The order itself had to be guarded with one's life. If the paper was torn or even scratched, the householder on whose door it hung was arrested.

It was decided by the District Congress that first Shyama and then, one week later, Janak would defy the orders that banned us from public activity. A procession was formed at the Congress office, and it grew as it wound its way through the city. It stopped at Anarkali Bazaar, where Shyama took over its leadership. She was arrested before she had walked a furlong. Several people, both men and women, were arrested with her, and, when the crowd refused to disperse, the police resorted to a *lathi*-charge.

Despite the fact that this was a peaceful demonstration, demonstrators did not always remain calm when being hit by *lathis*. Sometimes they retaliated, but then the police would open fire. Perhaps the government felt justified when this happened. I felt that if the British had behaved with greater foresight, the agitation would have died a natural death. By using violence on peaceful crowds and ordering indiscriminate arrests, they whipped up the demonstrators' enthusiasm even more and strengthened the crowd's determination to defy their orders.

Within a week, the same exercise was repeated by Janak. She too was arrested. My sisters stood for trial together and were sentenced to one year's rigorous imprisonment, which meant hard labor. They were fined one hundred rupees each. When they refused to pay, the police swooped down on our house and carried away the few odd chairs and some trunks we still had at home. Both Mother and I protested that the trunks contained our everyday apparel. The police would not listen, so my father wrote to the Punjab Government protesting such high-handed behavior. He said his daughters Janak and Shyama were of age and so had nothing to do with him. Their fines could be collected by freezing their bank accounts if they had them. This meant the authorities had to return whatever they had taken away. I had to go to the police station where the confiscated belongings were stored. I saw piles of carpets, furniture, and a large number of trunks that the police had collected from various homes in lieu of fines. I could not help gloating over the discomfort the police must have felt on being ordered to return our things. I told them that they should have heeded our warnings and not confiscated our belongings.

Meanwhile, a one month's grace given to Mother and me had expired. Another notice was pasted on the walls of our house for a further period of one month's good behavior. We decided that the time had come to defy this order. First, we spirited away the rest of our belongings and left the servants to guard the house. Then we went for our jail visit with Janak and Shyama, informing them that we would be joining them in a few days. Then Mother and I defied the order in the same way as had Janak and Shyama. At the trial, Mother was sentenced to two years of simple imprisonment and I was sentenced to one year's rigorous imprisonment.

This time there was no Gandhi–Irwin Pact to get us out of prison. Life was grim, and the twelve months seemed unending. On top of that, we were conscious that the general public was tired and the movement failing. It required a lot of courage and strength to disrupt a business, leave your home and family, and keep on going in and out of prison. Who was to look after the family? In our case we had our father. He never got actively involved in politics, though he wore *khadi* all his life. He had responsibilities to his wife and children and to Motilal's family as well.

Congress did not have the finances or the personnel to look after such families. Often, entire Congress committees were declared illegal, their offices raided, and all documents confiscated. Even if the All-India Congress Committee had had a protest scheme, there was no staff to carry it out. Besides, all the leaders, both those of consequence and the local leaders, had been arrested. The rank and file could not organize themselves without leadership.

The repressive measures were very severe. In villages, women were molested and raped, their menfolk beaten almost to death. The revolutionary movement had practically died out, partly because its leaders were either dead or in prison and partly because Gandhiji used to condemn it openly. I personally think that Gandhiji was wrong in believing that nonviolence was the only way to achieve freedom and that Congress was the only organization consisting of patriots. The young revolutionaries were the ones who really sacrificed. They lived in hiding, wary of everyone they met. And some died—like Bhagwati Charan, who was grievously wounded testing a bomb. He could not be taken to the hospital, nor could any doctor be entrusted with his identity, so he died without medical attention.

The third time we were in prison we again met Sushila Mohan. The daughter of a high-ranking army officer, she was a revolutionary with a high price on her head. She had changed her name to Sushila and courted arrest in Delhi as part of Gandhi's movement. Sentenced to six months' simple imprisonment she came to the Lahore Female Jail, where she shared our accommodation, that is, the one room four of us were already sharing with Aruna Asaf Ali. We guarded her carefully, hoping that fellow prisoners would not recognize her and inform the authorities. She had already served her six-month prison term and was still in prison in lieu of her fine. Then someone recognized her. Immediately Mother sent for a Congress worker and asked him to pay her fine and get her released. He brought a complete set of clothes—Punjabi dress of *shalwar-kameez* [trousers and a dress] (Sushila habitually wore saris) and dark glasses—when he came to secure her release.

For our hard labor we were given some needlework that we had to finish on the same day we received it. When our good friend Mrs. Bhola Nath visited us, we asked her to tell our friends outside to purchase whatever we had stitched—bed sheets, hand towels, and table cloths.

While we were still in prison, the Inspector General of prisons, Colonel Barker, came around for inspection. He found many young girls strolling about aimlessly in the evenings and this led him to ask the superintendent, Colonel P.D. Chopra, how we passed our evenings. Did we play any games? The answer was negative. The Inspector General immediately ordered that a couple of badminton courts be set up in the hospital compound, and the superintendent was enjoined to see that all the young women played in the evenings. He also sanctioned ceiling fans for the class A wards and the usual remission allowed hard labor prisoners. This meant that at the end of the year, our sentences were reduced by twenty-eight days. The movement was almost dead by this time we went to prison, and these eleven months were very boring. Gone was the enthusiasm of 1930 when new arrivals brought excitement to our otherwise dull and monotonous lives.

It was at this time that Durga Bhagwati Charan was brought to prison. She also had a price on her head. Her husband was dead and her comrade Bhagat Singh had been executed. Other comrades were in the Andaman Islands, serving long sentences. I think she had lost heart, and one evening she and a fellow revolutionary, Sampuran Singh Tandon, surrendered to the police. She was brought to prison late one night. We were strolling in the compound after dinner and out of sheer boredom were peering through the chink in the iron gate just to have a glimpse of the outside world. We were excited and surprised to see a large posse of police almost filling the jail premises. We guessed that someone of great importance had been arrested—but who could it be? Durga was already in the office so we could not see her. At last the wicket gate opened, and in stepped a slim and not very tall woman. She walked over to me and said in Hindustani, "Do you recognize me?" I hesitated for a moment and then said, "Yes, I do." Then she was whisked away. Because she was a revolutionary she was kept in a separate cell. She was not very communicative, though we all tried to engage her in conversation. I think it was only Satyavati who was able to draw her out. I do not remember how long she remained in our prison or when she was released. Although I had never met her before, I had guessed her identity correctly. The moment she was taken away to her cell, all my fellow prisoners asked me who she was and where I had met her.

Because of my activities in the student union, there were many who considered me a revolutionary. After our first release from prison, Father was warned by a high official of the Criminal Investigation Department (CID) that the authorities were planning to implicate me in some revolutionary activity and have me incarcerated in Lahore Fort. They planned to have a police stooge get up and greet me at one of the general meetings of the student union. My returning the greeting would be evidence enough of my association with the revolutionaries. My father was very worried. He impressed on me the danger of attending any public meetings of students. He said that Mother, alone in prison, would be very upset if I were taken to Lahore Fort. Fortunately, this police scheme came to naught and I continued with my activities in the student union.

At the end of their sentence, Janak and Shyama were released together. They left for Bombay to stay with our eldest sister, Chandra. I was released one month later; Mother had yet another year to go. We did not want to reopen the house just yet, so I stayed with Lala Pindi Das in Lahore. His wife and three daughters had been with us in prison. One evening we decided to go to the cinema on McLeod Road, and since it was not very far we decided to walk. There were eight to ten of us, both young women and young men, and, as all of us had at one time or another been in prison, each had a "tail" in the person of a CID man. So here we were, going to the cinema, with eight to ten CID men following us. Finally, we told them where we were going and suggested that only one of them accompany us; the rest could go home. They finally agreed. After staying with Lala Pindi Das for a few days,

I went to Allahabad to stay with Father. Later, Janak, Shyama, and I returned to Lahore and reopened our house on Panj Mohal Road. This was in 1933.

After being in and out of prison for three years, it was difficult to pick up the threads of a normal life. Shyama had given up the idea of studying for her master's, and mother had been released from prison after serving eighteen months, as her health was deteriorating rapidly. On her release, she went to Bombay for medical treatment. It seemed that a very important phase of our life was over. India had not achieved its goal of independence, but it had taught the people the value of concerted action. People showed an immense capacity for suffering in a dignified manner. At this time we gave up the house on Panj Mahal Road and rented a bungalow on Ferozepur Road, near Ichra. In the compound, there were three lovely houses with enough room for us and sizable lawns in front and back. The houses were newly built, so there was no hedge and no boundary wall. We occupied the middle house. The CID used to trouble us a lot, especially at night. At times they would turn off the main electric switch and leave us in complete darkness. Once one of them crept up the back verandah and tried to peep through the glass panes of the door. Mother had just returned from a Congress tour and we had a meeting of some workers at our house. Everyone left late at night. After bolting the front door, I was going to my room when I saw a man trying to look into the corridor. I shouted to my sister, unbolted the door, and ran after him, but he disappeared. As the movement gradually died out, these harassments also stopped.

Gandhiji decided to retire from politics for the time being and devote his attention to *harijan* welfare work. He started on an all-India tour, addressing meetings in different towns and organizing the work for the betterment of the *harijans*. He had planned a visit to Lahore as well. Women volunteers were again needed to keep order at his prayer meetings, both mornings and evenings, so Shyama and I offered our services. In Lahore the meetings were held in the compound of the Dayanand Anglo-Vedic (DAV) College. Mother, Shyama, and I had to get up at 2:30 A.M. to be at the college for the morning prayers at 4:00 A.M. Hearing this unusual commotion in the middle of the night, one of our neighbors inquired if there had been a burglary in the house. They were surprised that we were going to Gandhi's prayer meeting at that unearthly hour.

Gandhiji spent a week in Lahore, and for all those days we were on duty at the early morning prayer meetings as well as all his public meetings. As the weather was warm, the public, desirous of attending the morning prayer meeting, used to sleep either on the pavement outside the college premises or on the lawns so that they could be there in time. On one occasion, I saw a woman with a small sleeping baby whom she was trying to awaken. When I remonstrated with her, she said she wanted to be sure her child had Gandhiji's *darshan* [the experience of seeing Gandhi], for this might be his only opportunity. Such was the reverence for Gandhi.

At one of the public meetings a young bride lost her gold chain. Someone in the crowd had snatched it. When she discovered the loss, she became hysterical about what her mother-in-law would say. When Mother heard of this, she went to Gandhiji, told him of the young girl's plight, and asked him to give her a necklace from the jewelry he had collected for the *Harijan* Fund. He did so quite happily.

I think Gandhiji's tour was the last public event we had in Lahore. Otherwise, we led a normal life. Congress was devoting its time to *harijan* uplift and village industries work. There was nothing exciting for us to do and no reason to continue living in Lahore. So we finally moved back to Allahabad in March 1935. Our police records had been transferred there, and one of our police friends, Islam Ahmad, came and told Mother about this, remarking that, of the four sets of records, mine was the worst. But the Allahabad police had no reason to be wary of me; I left soon after to work in Bihar.

8

A New Life

The end of the *satyagraha* movement marked a turning point in my life. When we came out of prison, life was no longer full of exciting events. We had all finished our education (Shyama had abandoned plans to study for her master's degree, as I mentioned) so there was no reason to continue living in Lahore. At any rate, by this time Allahabad University had become one of the three or four finest teaching universities in the country and had thrown its doors open to women students.

Father decided that we should return to Allahabad, where we had a big house with extensive grounds of our own. Janak decided to leave by train, but Shyama and I, more adventurous, decided to go by car. We left Lahore early one morning in March 1935 and drove straight to Delhi, where we spent the night with Mr. and Mrs. Asaf Ali. We had a cousin, Anand Nehru, posted in Agra, so our next stop was with him. The third was at Kanpur, where one of my maternal uncles was posted. We finally reached Allahabad on the fourth day. Mother had stayed behind in Lahore to wind up our affairs and say good-bye to friends.

I had not given up the idea of teaching in a school, so as soon as I had settled down in Allahabad I asked Pandit Krishna Kant Malaviya* to find out about a position in Bihar. When Mother joined us, she announced my engagement to Amrit Lal Sahgal. He was a young

---

*Nationalist, social reformer, close associate of the Nehru family.

Punjabi, a chartered accountant whom we knew quite well in Lahore and whose family was known to us as well. Since his return from England in 1928, he had been very keen on marrying me. He was the first Punjabi, and the third Indian, to qualify as a chartered accountant trained in England. The wedding was fixed for sometime in winter, so I decided that if the teaching position I had heard about in Bihar was still open I would take it.

Ram Nandan Misra, the Bihar Congress leader, was delighted to have me take charge of his little village school. The journey to Bihar was long and tedious because we had to take a local train from Allahabad to Darbhanga, and from there a rickety car to the school, four miles into the interior of Laheria Sarai, a suburb of Darbhanga. Most of the children had never seen a car, and my arrival created a sensation.

My sojourn in Bihar was an unforgettable experience and one that I thoroughly enjoyed. It gave me firsthand knowledge of the backwardness of rural Bihar, especially of the condition of women and children. The school, called Bihar *Mahila Vidyapith* [Bihar Female School], was meant for village girls up to fifteen or sixteen years of age, but about thirty little boys were enrolled as well. Set in the rural countryside, it had mango groves and fields of sugarcane all around. The school was run on donations, so there were only two complete buildings. Most of the staff were men who lived there with their families in two-room flats. There were three women on staff: myself as the headmistress, a south Indian woman teacher named Kamla (her husband was also on staff), and a nurse. Parts of the two buildings housed the office and the classrooms, and half of each building was used as a dormitory, one for boys and the other for girls.

I was given two rooms in a half-finished third building. The floor was made of mud and the furniture was plain and simple: a wooden platform to sleep on, a table, a couple of chairs, and a small wooden platform on which to keep books and clothing. For my bath there was a sturdy room with a cement floor. Water had to be carried in a bucket from a well near the kitchen. Gandhiji's trench-style lavatories were used by everyone.

Life was hard but I enjoyed myself. I had our old servant, Janki, with me to do the cooking and household chores. There was no electricity, no road, and no social life, but there was a small library in a nearby ashram run by Congress workers. I used to borrow books from there and go to consult the *vaidji* [doctor of traditional medicine] about minor ailments. I even used to do a little doctoring myself. Late one night a girl complained of a severe earache. I was at my wits' end about what to do when it suddenly occurred to me to put two drops of warm glycerine in her ear. So I warmed it in a spoon over a candle flame and was as surprised as everyone else when it helped. The girl slept well and the next morning had no pain.

I soon became friends with Mrs. Misra, the wife of the Congress leader Ram Nandan Misra. Ram Nandan's father was a very wealthy *zamindar* [landlord] of that area, and his family's house could be glimpsed from the school grounds. Ram Nandan came under the influence of Mahatma Gandhi and began to work for village welfare on his father's estate. He was totally unsuccessful, however, and eventually left in disgust and joined the ashram at Wardha, but he had to leave his wife behind because his father was an extremely orthodox man and the women of the household lived in strict *purdah*. Gandhiji persuaded the young man to bring his wife from his father's home so she could work among the women. There was no way for Ram Nandan to get his father's permission for this, so he sent word to her to jump out of a particular window in the dead of night. He planned to meet her and take her by car to the nearest railway station and then to Wardha. The plan was successful, but the old *zamindar* was so angry that he disowned his son and daughter-in-law. Fortunately, they had no children at the time. I used to ask Mrs. Misra what would happen if we went to visit her mother-in-law and the other women of the family. She would laugh and say her husband would not hear of it.

Every morning the children walked a mile to the village pond to bathe. The village pond is known as *pokhar*, and all children learn to swim at an early age. Before I became headmistress, the boys and girls would go straight from their bath to the kitchen for breakfast and then immediately to morning prayers. No one asked them to tidy themselves or even comb their hair. I talked with the nurse about this, but she told me that there were too many girls with long hair for her to comb them all. I decided to call on the village barber. All the girls had their hair cut in the then fashionable bob; they looked so smart. One little girl had rows and rows of lice in her head, however, so I had her hair shaved off completely. With short hair, the younger girls were much easier for the nurse to look after. I decided that the children should sit for morning prayers at 7:30 A.M. and that when they did so they would be neat, clean, and orderly. Then school would start. Formerly, the organizers had run the school on the lines of the Wardha ashram, where prayers began between 5:00 A.M. and 6:00 A.M. I explained that since we were running a school, not an ashram, classes could begin with morning prayers at 7:30 A.M. During my tenure there I learned by heart the last eighteen verses of chapter 2 of the *Bhagavad Gita* [Song of the Lord]; they were Gandhiji's favorite and were recited by the entire school at both morning and evening prayers.

There was a big quadrangle enclosed by the three school buildings, so after school hours I used to teach the girls the games I had played in my childhood. The schoolmasters objected strongly, saying they did not like the idea of women running! I was very surprised, so I asked them what women they were referring to; these were only young girls. "Besides," I said, "who asked you to sit in the office after school hours and watch? Why don't you go home?" They were embarrassed, but I decided not to make an issue of it, so I took the girls to the nearby mango grove where they could run and shout to their hearts' content. No restrictions were placed on the boys, so they could play football on the school grounds.

The monsoons that year were exceptionally heavy, and the Kamla River, which ran close to the school, was flooded. For days we anxiously watched its progress as the water covered one field after another. We continued to hope we would be spared, but the day came when our school was also flooded. The floors of my rooms were made of clay, so they became damp and began to sink. For days we had to wade in muddy, knee-deep water, and there was nothing to eat except rice and *dal*. Fortunately I did not catch a chill or fall ill.

Dr. Rajendra Prasad, later the first President of the Republic of India, was then a well-known and respected Congress leader. He was affiliated with Bihar, and, because this school was founded by a dedicated group of Congress workers, he came to pay us a visit and see for himself how we were making out during the flood.

Child marriages were prevalent in Bihar at that time. On my evening walks I used to be amazed to see little child wives of five or six years with *sindur* [red powder] smeared in the parting of their hair. This was a sign that the husband was still living, and it is still practiced by many Hindu women. The only redeeming feature of the child marriage system was that the bridegroom returned home alone after the wedding. The little bride was left with her parents for a few years, until she was older and could understand what married life meant. Then there was a second ceremony, called the *gauna*, when the bridegroom came to fetch his bride. The *gauna* ceremony was widely practiced in the Hindi-speaking areas of India, such as Uttar Pradesh, Madya Pradesh, Bihar, and Rajasthan. The only drawback of these early marriages was the possibility that something might happen to the bridegroom and that he might die before the *gauna* ceremony. The poor young girl would became a widow although she had never really been a wife.

The only festival I remember celebrating in Bihar was *Diwali*; we floated little lighted oil lamps on the pond near the school. The floating lamps looked very picturesque in those surroundings, with a clear, star-studded sky above and trees and green plants all around. It is something that I have never forgotten.

The school recessed for one month in July for summer vacation, and I went home to Allahabad. Before I left I sent a circular to all the parents requesting that they send what I considered the barest necessities—four saris, four sets of bed linen, and so forth—for their wards when school reopened. Not being conversant with the prejudices of rural Bihar, I also asked for one pair of *chappals* [leather sandals] for each boy and girl. What a sensation this created! Ram Nandan Misra received protest letters from the parents. Where did the headmistress come from? Who was she? Did she not know that the women of Bihar avoided leather footwear? In fact, any kind of footwear was taboo. Only the men were permitted to wear shoes. Misraji pacified them by canceling the request for footwear.

Before the summer vacation, Mother came to see me and we visited some dignitaries of Muzaffarnagar and Patna to see what havoc the earthquakes had created.* During our travels, we had to cross the Ganges in a steamer to reach the railhead at Mokamahghat. I had never before seen the broad expanse of this river. The Ganges in Allahabad shrank to almost nothing when there was no rain, but here the river was deep enough for the steamers to ply.

When I returned to school after summer vacation, I stayed on in Bihar until November, and then, after a short visit to my eldest sister, Chandra, in Calcutta, I returned to Allahabad. I have always been intensely interested in our country's social problems and my experience with that small village school provided invaluable insights. It

---

*Bihar experienced a series of earthquakes in 1935.

certainly widened my horizons and gave me a different perspective from that of many women my age.

I often wonder what happened to that school and to the girls studying there. Ram Nandan Misra and his wife came to my wedding, but after that we completely lost touch. Some years later I heard a rumor that Misraji had left the Congress and joined the Socialist party. After my marriage, I ceased to be actively associated with Congress until after Independence, so I was unable to check with anyone in Bihar as to what had happened to my old friends. Life for me changed completely.

I was married on December 24, 1935. Because my husband had joined the Government of India in the Ministry of Commerce, as the Secretary of the newly formed Indian Accountancy Board, we lived in New Delhi. Nothing had prepared me for life as a government servant's wife in the capital city.

9

New Delhi and Simla

We had hardly settled down in our house at 6 Dupleix Lane when my husband was ordered to proceed to Burma, then part of the British Empire. I accompanied him and had my first taste of a sea voyage. Unfortunately, I was not a good traveler in those days, so my three days on board the steamer were very trying. I was indeed happy to see the sampans on the Irrawaddy River as we neared the coast of Rangoon. We spent three days in Rangoon, and when my husband was not working, we visited all the sights, including the famous Shwe-de-gong Pagoda and of course all the shops. We then returned to Delhi.

One of my husband's duties was to keep in touch with all the practicing accountants all over the country and to help solve their problems. These were then discussed at the annual meeting of the Indian Accountancy Board held in December in New Delhi. He had to tour all the major cities in India to meet the British-qualified chartered accountants, as well as Indians trained in India as incorporated accountants and registered accountants. What the difference were among these three categories I am afraid I do not know. All I know is that one had to go abroad to obtain the degree of chartered accountant. Whenever the board met, our house became the center of social activities.

Learning to be a government official's wife was not easy for me. I think it must have been in 1936 when Lord Willingdon relinquished his charge as Governor General and Viceroy of India. He and Lady Willingdon were leaving by train for Bombay, where they would board a ship back to Great Britain. All officers of all ranks—both British and Indian—were required to see them off. Having a strong Congress background and personal experience with the repressive measures formulated by Lord Willingdon, I was in no mood to go to the New Delhi railway station to bid him bon voyage. But my husband's sister reminded me that I was now married to a government servant and should do as the other wives were doing, that is, go to the railway station.

It so happened that King George VI had passed away a few months earlier and the Court was still in mourning. Women were expected to wear black or white or lavender. I am afraid I had never given a thought to the phrase "the Court is in mourning." As I was newly married, I thought the farewell at the station would be a wonderful opportunity to show off one of my saris. I gaily donned a strawberry-colored silk sari and went off with my sister-in-law. My husband was not present as he had quietly slipped away to the club for a rubber of bridge. He did not believe in observing these formalities, and even after Independence I had to drag him to the President's receptions at *Rashtrapati Bhavan* (the President's residence). Needless to say, I created a sensation at the New Delhi railway station. Everyone was scandalized to see me dressed in such a bright color. Afterward, my sister-in-law bore a lot of criticism for not instructing me about the approved colors to wear.

Amrit was in the Ministry of Commerce, so he was constantly being transferred to Calcutta for long periods to serve as a member of the Tariff Board for all inquiries on textiles, jute, and sugar. During the first inquiry, which was soon after we were married, we stayed with my sister Chandra and her husband in Calcutta. It was there that I came to know of the International Council of Women, which was holding its triennial congress there. I worked with the social workers of Calcutta on the arrangements for the conference and thereby found out about the Indian Branch of the International Council of Women—The National Council of Women in India (NCWI), which had been founded in 1925. On my return to Delhi, I immediately joined the Delhi branch and visited nearby rural areas with other members, both Indian and foreign. This group never took up concrete work, perhaps because of the seasonal shifts, but concentrated on providing the services of a nurse-*dai* [trained midwife] to the women in rural Delhi. That was about all we did. It gave me an opportunity to meet most of the British women, wives of secretaries to the Government of India.

New Delhi in those days was very different from the New Delhi of today. On December 12, 1911, King Emperor George V transferred the capital of India from Calcutta to Delhi. Temporary buildings were erected in the old civil lines north of the city in 1912 as residences for the officers. But these were temporary measures only. Clearly, "old Delhi" would not make a suitable capital city. So a new site, known as Raisina, about two and a half miles south of the northern wall of Shahjahanabad, as the old walled city was then called, was selected for the new capital. The tasks of designing and planning New Delhi were given to two British architects: Sir Edward Lutyens and Sir Herbert Baker. The construction was delayed by World War I, so New Delhi was not formally declared open until 1930. It had been occupied, however, since 1923–24, when old Delhi was visited by floods.

New Delhi is a planned city. At the highest point on Raisina Hill stands the imposing Viceregal Lodge (now *Rashtrapati Bhavan*). It is flanked by two great Central Secretariat buildings. Designed by Sir Herbert Baker, these buildings are known as the North and South Blocks. The houses surrounding the Viceroy's house and the Secretariat buildings were laid out with extensive lawns.

The whole of New Delhi is very symmetrical in design. All streets, roads, roundabouts, and houses were built on more or less the same lines. The cream-colored exteriors of the buildings were picturesque but also a source of great confusion for the residents. For those without a strong sense of direction, it was easy to get lost in New Delhi.

The main shopping center was and still is Connaught Place, named after the Duke of Connaught. The original Connaught Place consisted of an inner circle and an outer circle, but it has grown much larger and now extends in various directions. The planners wanted the shoppers to be free to move from shop to shop in all weather—rain or shine—through spacious corridors. New Delhi then was a city in itself. Meant exclusively for the government of India and its officers, it was very much an imperial city.

The government actually had two capitals. For six months of the year, the entire government moved to Simla to escape the heat. The winter capital was, of course, New Delhi. The movement of the entire government with all their personnel as well as documents, files, and records to a cooler climate was a practice unique to India. I viewed it as a colossal waste of money carried out with total disregard for public opinion. The All-India Congress was very critical of these moves, but their criticism had no effect until many years later. In addition to the official records, the personal belongings of all the officers, senior and junior, had to be transferred as well. The system employed for this move was very efficient. Officers were moved in two groups, with one week between the moves. Days before the move, each officer had to indicate whether he was going in the first group or the second; all arrangements were made accordingly. The contractor in charge of moving our baggage would send his men, with transportation, to our house to collect what we were taking and deliver it at the other end. Because we were going for six months, we had to take all our household goods—silverware, crockery, cutlery, kitchen utensils, carpets, and so forth, as well as all our clothing and personal effects. Eventually, we became so experienced at moving that not one package was lost or misplaced. I do not know how the other wives felt, but this constant shuffling every six months used to give me the most unsettled feeling. No sooner did you feel at home in one place than it was time to pack and move again.

Simla was the seat not only of the central government, but of the Punjab Government as well. Simla East, or "*Chota* [small] Simla" as it was called, was more or less reserved for the Punjab Government, which had its own Secretariat Building, Government House, and residences for officials. The rest of Simla accommodated the Government of India with the Viceregal Lodge, the Central Legislative Building, and the Secretariat buildings. The Central Legislative Building was the same one in front of which I had organized a demonstration in 1930 against the Viceroy Lord Irwin. Now I saw it through different eyes. The Viceroy's residence was an imposing building. The senior officers, most of whom were British, had houses allocated to them according to their designation and rank. Junior officers, like my husband, had to fend for themselves. Not knowing very much about the geography of Simla, we had booked a set of rooms at Longwood, a hostel for the members of the Central Legislature, as a temporary measure until we could look around and find suitable accommodations.

The trip by car from Delhi was most uncomfortable, and the hilly road made me carsick. I was so sick that we had to halt at Solan for quite some time before I was able to continue the journey. Going from Kalka to Simla was quite a nightmare for me, and I was pleased when

Congress convinced the Government of India to leave some officers in New Delhi for the summer.

We did reach Simla, but I found very little peace in Longwood. It was also quite a distance from the mall. The day after arriving we set out to look for a house and, as luck would have it, we found a ground-floor flat in a very nice house called "Rookville" near the United Services Club and not far from the mall. It had four bedrooms as well as living and dining rooms. What was most attractive about that house was the huge L-shaped glass-enclosed verandah—ideal for the Simla weather, especially during monsoons. My husband's father, his aunt, and three sisters came from Lahore to spend the hot weather with us, so the house was full. One of my husband's sisters, Padma Bhandari, rented the Rookville Cottage just below us, so her children spent most of their time with us. Because I love walking in the hills, the location of this house was ideal. The upstairs flat was occupied by people we knew, which helped to create a pleasant atmosphere.

In 1937, we returned from Simla to take up residence in 6 Duplex Lane. Amrit's next assignment on the Tariff Board was in Calcutta. Fortunately we were able to find a furnished flat with telephone facilities on Park Street in Calcutta for two hundred rupees per month. Our accommodations included a huge drawing room, a double bedroom with a dressing room and attached bath, a south verandah, which served as a dining room, a kitchen, a pantry, and servant quarters for the cook and baby's* *ayah* [nursemaid]. It was attached to a boarding house run by an Anglo-Indian woman. For transportation she had placed her own car—an Austin 10—with a driver at our disposal. This required an additional monthly fee, plus whatever we spent on fuel. When I compare these rates with present-day prices, I am amazed at our good fortune. To find such a well-furnished flat in this location was nothing short of a miracle. My sister Janak came to Calcutta to buy a car for herself and drove back to Allahabad with a chauffeur in attendance. Chandra came from Rangoon with her two daughters, Rajana and Nona. At that time we rented another bedroom for her on the same floor. Her boat had been involved in a severe cyclone, so she arrived looking very battered and far from well. She rested for a few days before leaving for Allahabad. My son Pradip was just learning to

---

*The author's son, Pradip, was born in 1937.

crawl, to the intense excitement of Rajana, who was nine years old, and Nona, who was only two—just a baby herself.

While in Calcutta we attended horse races at the main racecourse and at Tollygang and Barrackpore. Because Barrackpore was some distance from Calcutta, we took Baby Pradip with us and left him with the driver and the *ayah* while we went to watch the races. On another occasion we drove to Chandernagar, then still a French settlement. In Calcutta we visited the Victoria Memorial and the Jain temple. Calcutta was a British-oriented city then. Since it had been the capital of India about twenty-five years previously, all the big business houses had their headquarters there. Chowringee Street was the promenade for society people with the *maidan* [level area of ground] and the Victoria Memorial forming a backdrop.

The All-India Congress Committee met in Calcutta that year. With my husband's permission I attended the sessions. There I met Jawahar Bhai, who complained that I had not been to see him. He told me he was staying with Subash Chandra Bose at their family house at Woodburn Park and asked me to meet him there. I went one evening, but the Working Committee was in session. I waited for a long time, hoping that the meeting would be over soon. Finally, at about 9:00 P.M. Subash Bose came out and informed me that the deliberations had been prolonged, so I would not be able to meet Jawahar Bhai. In those days Jawaharlal still cared about family ties, as his courtesy in sending me that message shows.

On our return from Simla in October 1938 we were allotted 7 Canning Lane—one of the houses reserved for the members of the Central Legislature—as a temporary accommodation. The security arrangements in those days were so good that we were able to leave our belongings in the hands of the contractor, depart Simla by car for a visit to Lahore, and arrive later in Delhi without giving a thought to the safety of our belongings. The baggage had been handed over to the contractor as usual at Simla to be delivered to 7 Canning Lane. When we arrived in Delhi we found every piece intact in the custody of the Central Public Works Division (CPWD) *chowkidar* [guard].

I soon became interested in the construction of what is now called the Birla temple. Raja Baldeo Dass Birla, a major industrialist, had decided to construct a temple dedicated to Lakshmi [goddess of wealth] and her consort Narayan. Constructed of red sandstone, the temple blends well with Rashtrapati Bhavan and the Secretariat Building. The temple complex consists of a Gita Bhavan, where religious discourses are held, a *dharamshala* [shelter] for the pilgrims coming from outside, and a beautifully planned lawn with streams and caves. The idols were made by artisans from Rajasthan and from marble that came from the famous quarries of Makrana in the same state. I was a frequent visitor to the construction site. When the temple was declared open by Gandhiji at an impressive ceremony before a large gathering, I was present. I then became a regular visitor to the temple and came to know all the *purjaries* [priests] and others who staffed the temple.

At about this time I came into contact with the Delhi Branch of the Sri Ramkrishna Mission and came to know the secretary, Swami Kailasanand, very well. The mission was much smaller than it is nowadays, and the beautiful temple of Sri Ramkrishna and the library/auditorium building are post-Independence additions. In those days, the mission was housed in a single building with a shrine on the second floor. Visitors used to go upstairs to pray or meditate before coming down to meet the Swami. Now the temple is a building by itself. The last time I saw Swami Kailasanand was when he was transferred to Madras. He stopped off in Bombay en route, and I went to pay my respects to him. We had lunch together, which was somewhat embarrassing as I was served by the Swamis instead of doing the serving myself.

There were very few schools in Delhi in those days. The best known were the Presentation Convent near the main railway station, the Jesus and Mary Convent, and St. Columbus School for boys. The Modern School, emphasizing new techniques and method of education, had its own buildings at Barakhamba Road. It owed its origin to a visionary and a philanthropist—Raghubir Singh. He came from an old and wealthy Delhi family. The Modern School was unique because it offered other amenities—riding and swimming, for example—besides the usual sports. These extras were part of the curriculum, so the school had longer hours and children who went there left home early in the morning and returned late in the evening.

Preprimary schools were rare. A friend of ours, Jawan Lal Gauba, the younger son of the noted Punjabi industrialist, Lala Harkishan Lal, came to settle in Delhi in the 1930s. His German wife, Elizabeth, started a small private nursery school in her own home for her friends' children. My two older children, Pradip and Anjali, began their schooling there. Actually, Anjali started going to school in Srinagar in 1941 when both the children were admitted to the Presentation Convent there. As we were living in a houseboat opposite the guest house, they used to go to school in a *shikara* [small boat] instead of a car.

New Delhi was not a very cultured city in those days. There were few academic or cultural facilities. I had learned to play the sitar before I was married and found there was a music teacher called Master Mohan who taught both vocal and instrumental music to the wards of the Indian officers. Master Mohan moved back and forth between New Delhi and Simla when the government of India moved so as not to disrupt the lessons of his pupils. For some reason I disliked him, though, and would not accept him as my sitar tutor. At that time no other music teacher was prepared to come from Darya Ganj in old Delhi for just one pupil. I had a similar difficulty in finding a pandit to coach me in Sanskrit. I had some knowledge of the language, having studied it for my intermediate examination in college, and wanted to continue. But between Darya Ganj in old Delhi and Hardinge Bridge (now Tilak Bridge) was a no man's land. The only building of note was the district jail. This prison had hallowed memories for me, as all our Delhi Congress leaders, Dr. M.A. Ansari, Asaf Ali, Deshbandhu Gupta, and Maulana Abul-Kalam Azad, had been incarcerated there at one time or another during the freedom struggle. The women from Delhi who had shared our prison life in Lahore were also housed there for a few days prior to their transfer to the Lahore Jail. The Delhi Conspiracy Case prisoners had made this jail famous. Every morning during their trial, before the court got down to its routine, these young men used to sing a very stirring national song in Hindi. The words of this song haunt me even now. After Independence the prison was moved to a building beyond the Delhi cantonment and is now known as the Tehar Jail. The old building was razed, and new buildings have been built to house the Maulana Azad Medical College. There was no public transport between old and New Delhi, and little to entice teachers to travel by foot or by bicycle.

In 1939 we were living on Kushak Road. I found this so far away from the city and so lonely that my husband requested other accomodations. On our return from Simla that year we were told to move to 6 Raisina Road, next to the Chelmsford Club. That year we had decided to go up to Simla with the second group, as we had booked rooms at the Clarke's Hotel. I was sitting at home one evening when the servants brought to my notice the fact that we were the only family in residence within a radius of five miles. All the other officers and their families had already gone, presumably in the first group. Even the Commander-in-Chief, whose official residence was what is now known as Teen Murthi House, had also left Delhi. New Delhi was so far-flung that areas like Kushak Road were not considered very safe. In addition, our grounds were large, with the servants' quarters some distance from the main house. I became so alarmed on hearing this that I hurriedly packed, handed over the baggage to the contractor and the possession of the house to the CPWD, and moved out. We had opted to go to Simla in the latter group, however, so we had to await our turn in the train. For the few days that we stayed in Delhi we moved in with my sister Janak and her husband, who had rented a small house on Asmanpur Road behind Maiden's Hotel in old Delhi.

The house on Raisina Road was a boon in more ways than one. Besides being very centrally located, it was next to the Chelmsford Club. In those days the hedge served as a boundary. My husband was very fond of bridge and he found his evening relaxation at the club, while the children could use the swimming pool. It was the best thing that could have happened to us.

It was at this time that the government modified its "two capitals" policy. Congress had been criticizing the Delhi–Simla move for years as a colossal waste of money. To placate them, the Government of India decided to move only a small number of offices to Simla. All ancillary departments, like my husband's, which had nothing to do with direct administration of the country, were ordered to stay in Delhi. Personally, I was relieved that we did not have to spend every summer in Simla. I am fond of travel and could now visit Musoorie or Kashmir during the hot weather; of course, I could not be away for six months, but a change for a couple of months was more than enough, and we were able to lead a more settled life.

Air-conditioning was unheard of then, but some comfort to mitigate the heat had to be provided. The government put up *khas tatties* [woven mats] in our home and provided the services of a man to keep them wet. As the air passed through these mats it cooled. At night we slept on the lawn. New Delhi had been designed as a garden city, with lovely trees and green lawns, so the hot weather was not as tiresome as it is now. Sleeping right out in the open was quite comfortable. Mosquitoes had been eradicated and, in spite of the proximity of the Rajasthan Desert, the *loo* [hot wind] was practically nonexistent. The weather seemed more predictable then than it is now. Winters used to be more prolonged and far more severe, and the rains came when they were expected. I remember having fires in the living room even during the daytime.

The triennial session of the National Council of Women in India (NCWI) was held in New Delhi in the winter of 1939. Lady Protima Mitter, the wife of Sir B.L. Mitter, Law Secretary, was the Chair, and my sister Janak was Secretary. During my years in Simla, 1936–39, I was the Secretary of the Simla branch of the All-India Women's Conference (AIWC) when Rajkumari Amrit Kaur was the President. She and I remained friends until the time of her death. We were instrumental in getting the Simla Municipal Committee to provide raincoats for the ricksha pullers. We also persuaded the Municipal Committee to build a children's park with a swing, a seesaw, and jungle gyms.

One custom peculiar to the government in those days was the "ladies' parties" it encouraged. These were frequently thrown by wives of the Indian members of the Viceroy's Executive Council who observed *purdah* and did not attend any official functions at the Viceroy's house or elsewhere. These "ladies' parties" were for women only. I was a frequent visitor at the parties hosted by Lady Jagdish Prasad and Lady Sultan Ahmed. These parties were very enjoyable as the atmosphere was relaxed and more often than not there was impromptu singing and dancing. Tea was served by women servants. Lady Jagdish Prasad's two daughters were students at Indraprastha College, where they were taught by my sister Janak, then on the staff as an English professor.

In 1939 my sister Chandra and her husband were in Rangoon. My brother-in-law, Sri Krishna Handoo, was with the Imperial Bank, and, because Burma was also a part of India, he had been transferred there. They were not expecting to come back to India until sometime after 1939, so Chandra invited Mother and me to visit them. We accepted and left our accommodations in Simla. My husband moved in with a cousin of his, Bashi Ram, who had a house in Chota Simla, and I took the two children—Pradip, aged two and a half years, and Anjali, barely fifteen months old—and together with Mother left for Calcutta en route to Rangoon. My youngest daughter, Saloni, had not yet been born. There were only two large steamers for passenger service, and the voyage took three days. I was terribly seasick, and so was Mother. The *ayah* was no better, so it was up to the steward to look after the two young children as best he could. We stayed in Rangoon for about three months. The Second World War was imminent then, and my husband was terribly worried because he did not know how to get us back home. There was no air service, so the sea route was the only way, but there was the danger that the steamer might be bombed. Mother preferred to go home by a later boat, so I traveled alone with the children. Instead of plying a straight course, we zigzagged, so the trip took us an extra day at sea. We ran short of food and water, but the journey home was better than the journey out because I did not feel seasick. Fortunately, we reached Calcutta on the afternoon of the fourth day. I was met by some friends and stayed with them for a couple of days before proceeding to Allahabad and then on to Delhi.

The Second World War started on September 3, 1939. Before committing itself to the war effort, Congress wanted the British Government to spell out in plain words how far they were prepared to go to meet the aspirations of the Indian people. But the government replies were vague. Congress then started individual *satyagraha* (this was in 1942) as a protest against the country's being dragged into the war. Certain people were asked to come forward and court arrest.

I was now married to a government servant, so I did not join this movement. Aruna Asaf Ali had defied the government, but had no intention of courting arrest. She felt she would be more useful outside prison, so she went underground to continue working for India's freedom. During this time she sent word to me that she would like to stay with us for three or four days. Neither my husband nor I hesitated in welcoming her, but we were well aware of the risks we were taking. Had it been discovered that we were harboring an absconder, my husband would have been dismissed from service, and both of us would have been imprisoned as well. Aruna stayed with us at 6 Raisina Road, living the normal life of a houseguest, except we were careful not to call her by her real name nor let anyone else catch more than a glimpse of her.

In 1940 my husband joined the newly formed Income Tax Appellate Tribunal and was transferred from the Ministry of Commerce to the Ministry of Finance. This tribunal was a new venture on the part of the central government. It provided an opportunity for the general public to appeal if they were not satisfied with the decisions of their respective commissioners of income tax. Originally there were six members of the tribunal: three accountants and three lawyers. My husband, a chartered accountant, formed one bench with the President of the tribunal, Justice Munir. The Second World War was already on, and more and more accommodations were needed for defense personnel in New Delhi. It was therefore felt necessary to transfer all surplus officers, like the Income Tax Appellate Tribunal, which had no direct bearing on the war effort. So we were ordered to proceed to Bombay. There would be no bench in Delhi for the duration of the war, but the third bench would be located in Allahabad. My husband remained with the tribunal until he resigned from government service in July 1959, except for two years when he served as the Chair of the Delhi Central Electric Power Authority immediately after Partition. This was the first nationalized concern in the country.

My husband was not very happy about the transfer as he hated being uprooted from the place and the life he had become used to, but I have always loved traveling and visiting new places. I do not believe one can get to know a place and local customs without living there for some length of time. Bombay was and still is a very big industrial town. I had been there on a visit but had never lived there for any length of time. I looked forward to getting to know this new place.

We left Delhi in November 1942. I stayed on in Lahore for some time and then in Allahabad for a couple of months while Amrit looked for a flat. There were strong rumors in Allahabad that my father and Mohan Bhai (Mohanlal Nehru, another nephew of Motilal) were to be arrested. Mohan Bhai was constantly in and out of prison, leaving the administration of *Anand Bhavan* to my father. Mrs. Motilal was in frail health at this time, and Father used to visit her every evening. I also used to sit with her in the evening, as did my mother. She was the only grandmother I had known and my sisters and I were all very fond of her. I am sorry that no one has thought fit to write about her, for she shouldered a great deal of responsibility. She had her own children as well as the children of three of her husband's siblings to bring up, educate, marry, and launch into life. She experienced radical changes in her own life-style. First, the family became very Westernized: eating Western food, wearing shoes and stockings, and speaking English. Then there was the sudden swing over to extreme austerity and a simple mode of life under Gandhiji's influence. How did she feel when her husband and son were constantly in and out of prison? Her lovely house was gradually deprived of all its carpets and furnishings as the police took these for nonpayment of fines. She was never very robust in health. At times, with the menfolk away, *Anand Bhavan* would become as silent as the grave. I have always felt that her contribution to the freedom struggle was no less than that of her husband and son.

The authorities had a vague inkling that either my father or Mohan Bhai were handling the finances at *Anand Bhavan*, but they could not be certain. One cold January morning in 1943 the police swooped down on Mohan Bhai's house, next door to ours. I first heard about it from my children's *ayah* when she came on duty. I hurriedly woke up my parents, and all three of us walked over to Mohan Bhai's house. I remember that Pradip was nearly six and Anjali four and a half. They were very excited about these goings-on and came and sat at Mohan Bhai's gate. Nothing was discovered, however, so the authorities decided not to raid my father's house. But what a scare he had! He used to note down all major items of expenditure relating to *Anand Bhavan* in an innocuous looking small notebook, and every night he hid it in a different place.

10

Bombay, 1942–47

Before moving to Bombay, we went first to Lahore for a short vacation. From there my husband left directly for Bombay, and I moved on to Allahabad to stay with my parents until suitable accommodations could be found for the family. My younger daughter was barely a few months old at the time.

In Bombay we were lucky to find a very nice, commodious flat on the fourth floor of a building called Alcazar on Comballa Hill. It was situated on a small street called Navroji Gamadia Road, which linked Pedder Road and Warden Road (now called Bhulabhai Desai Road in honor of the veteran Congress leader).

In those days there were no high-rise buildings. The fourth floor was considered high enough to catch any breeze coming from the sea. It was a quiet, friendly place, and I soon got to know my neighbors, all of whom were very nice. The Shirazis, a family who had fled from Singapore in the wake of the war, lived just opposite, and we became especially fond of them. My children easily found playmates as there were children of all ages in the neighborhood. Among their close friends were children whose parents were Khojas [a branch of Shi'ite Muslim] from Sind. The Khoja family, the Sonawalas, thought that we were orthodox Hindus. Mr. Sonawala once mentioned that they gave my younger daughter Saloni only fruit to eat whenever she visited them so as not to offend us. I laughed and said that we did not mind what she ate. That broke the ice and brought us much closer to each other. After that I would go and have coffee with Mrs. Sonawala. The two or three British families in the neighborhood kept to themselves.

The Shirazi girls would come over and decorate our flat during *Diwali*. In those days, one could buy fresh mango leaves tied on a string at the market. All one had to do was to purchase as many feet of string as was needed and just put them up. Mango leaves are considered very auspicious—one puts them up on all important occasions like marriages and festivals, for example. On holidays my husband sometimes used to take the two older Shirazi girls (there were four of them), Begum and Alee, to the movies. For the *Eid* [Muslim holiday] celebrations, we would go their house.

Every Saturday morning we took the children to Crawford Market to buy toys while I did my shopping for vegetables. As I always encouraged my children to read, we used to go to a big book shop called Taraporewala, where I would select books for them. We soon had quite a collection, and although Pradip and Anjali liked reading books by themselves, my youngest, Saloni, preferred listening to books read aloud.

I found a very good private school called Hill Grange, on Pedder Road, for my children. It was run by two Parsi women, and the classes were from kindergarten to standard 6. The periods were a half-hour long and covered all the important subjects: English, arithmetic, history, and geography. French was taught as well. The children were home by lunchtime. Although the school was within walking distance, my knowledge of the heavy rains during the monsoon made me opt for the school bus both ways. Hindi was not in the curriculum, so I engaged a Hindi tutor, Pravin Chandra. He never bothered with the alphabet, the usual method of teaching, but started the children straight off on a book of easy words, thus making them gradually conversant with the alphabet. He was with us for all five years we were in Bombay. His method of teaching made the language interesting, and the children were able to take the Hindi examination organized by the *Hindi Prachar Sabha* [Society to Promote Hindi]. They passed with flying colors.

Saloni was barely eight months old when I arrived in Bombay. A young Indian chemist had carefully studied the diet of small babies and he used to prepare fresh cow's milk to which he had added sugar, extra fat, and vitamins. He then supplied bottles of the milk to his customers with small children. The milk was prepared very hygienically, and I used it with the utmost certainty that it was safe.

As soon as Saloni was three or four years old I got her admitted to the Hill Grange School. The staff had a novel method of teaching such small children. Parents had to send an attendant with the child. This attendant sat outside the school buildings on the lawn, while the child sat in the class. No restrictions were placed on the children; they were free to get up and go out, and free to play whenever they felt like it. That is where the personal attendant was needed. The attendant had to look after her charge and persuade the child in her care to go inside and sit in the class. The school had two rabbits in a large cage for the children to play with. The school authorities felt that it was necessary for the children to get used to the atmosphere of the school before they could settle down in their class. And it worked!

On one occasion my son Pradip told me that he had learned to speak and write both English and Hindi fluently and questioned the sense of continuing in school. There was a small shop near us that sold general items, called Rex Stores. I asked Pradip that now he felt his education was complete whether he would like to work at the Rex Stores? I mentioned that if I asked them they would perhaps agree to pay him ten rupees per month. He happily agreed!

Much against my husband's wishes, I made my son join the Cub Scouts. On one occasion the Cubs were being taken to Poona to camp, and their train left Bombay at midnight. My husband could not bear the thought that his only son might not get a full night's rest, so he wanted him to leave his companions and come home. He was after me not to let Pradip go to this camp; even at the railway station he kept on asking me to call him back, but I would not listen. I always felt, and still do, that children should not be mollycoddled or they will not be able to face hardships in life. So I said "Why don't you ask him yourself?" He did, but Pradip was not prepared to leave his companions. He had been looking forward to attending this camp for a long time, so we left him and returned home.

Unfortunately, Poona had a severe storm accompanied by heavy rainfall the next day. We were both very worried, but my husband was especially so. Although I knew the scoutmaster would remove the children to a safe place, I telephoned my cousin Bhuppi Atal, the manager of the Bank of India in Poona, to find out the details and let me know. He phoned back later to report that the boys were safe and were being well looked after. But the storm meant that Pradip's first camping experience, at the age of eight or nine years, was not entirely a happy one.

The public transport system in Bombay was by far the best I had seen so far. In those days, New Delhi had no such system. Since the New Delhi population moved every six months, and only government servants were housed there, I suppose buses were not needed, though tram cars were seen in some parts of old Delhi. When I settled down in Bombay I wanted to learn the major localities, so I would board a bus at Warden Road and get off at the Opera House of Churchgate or Colaba, walk around, and then travel home again by bus. When my little girl Saloni was able to walk, I used to take her with me. The conductors were very helpful and polite. They would always carry my little daughter boarding or getting off the bus. Her favorite ride was a buggy ride from the Imperial Bank of India to the *swadeshi* stores on Fheroze Shah Mehta Road. These buggies, horse-drawn carriages known as Victorias, cost half a rupee.

People from the suburbs used to commute to Bombay by train, a reliable and comfortable conveyance. Sometimes I took my children for a train ride from the Grant Road Station to Andheri—the last suburb in those days—and back again. Once the children and I went from Breach Candy bus stop to the terminal, just for a ride, and returned by another bus.

These were my days of experimenting with new activities. A nephew of mine was in the navy and in training in Bombay. On his days off he took me yachting. I enjoyed it thoroughly and was never seasick. Once there was a ship anchored some distance from the Gateway of India* whose captain knew my nephew. He invited us to tea on board the ship and sent his launch to the Gateway of India to pick us up. To board the ship one had to use a rope ladder. My two older children, Pradip and Anjali, were helped by the sailors, but I had to go up that rope ladder alone—dressed in a sari. How difficult that was! Coming down was much worse, because the rope ladder was not steady and the launch waiting below was rolling on the waves.

The Willingdon Club was within walking distance from our flat on Gamadia Road, so I decided to learn to swim. When I first started my

---

*Erected to commemorate the landing of King George V and Queen Mary in 1911 in their much-celebrated visit to India.

lessons we had an American coach. He never entered the pool to show newcomers various strokes but walked alongside the pool giving verbal directions. It was rumored that he had appeared in some men's figure competitions in New York and was very proud of his physique, which I presume meant he wanted to show off to the group of women he was coaching. After a few months he disappeared. The gossip was that someone had notified the American authorities in Bombay that there was a young man who was avoiding conscription for the war (the Second World War was in full swing, and the United States had joined the Allies). Whatever the reason, we never saw him again. Thus ended my first attempt to be a swimmer. After the war was over I found another coach at the swimming pool. It turned out that he was a retired British naval officer. So I promptly signed up for lessons, along with Pradip and Anjali. Our new coach, Mr. Johnson, did not hesitate to enter the pool to correct his pupils. After some months I became such a good swimmer that I could swim twenty-two lengths of that pool without stopping, quite an achievement for me. Of course, once I got a little confidence I used to put in a lot of practice in the mornings when the pool was not so crowded. Swimming became my son's favorite pastime, which he continued in the Doon School of Dehra Dun, where he was awarded a life-saving medal.

It was at this time that I became the General Secretary of the NCWI, which was an affiliate of the International Council of Women. Our President was Maharani Setu Parvati Bai of Travancore, and the Chair was Mrs. Tarabai Premchand, who also lived in Bombay. The NCWI had branches in all the major cities of India. I had first learned of the NCWI in Calcutta, so when I arrived in Bombay it was not new to me. The council defined itself as a social welfare organization removed from political concerns, but we could not ignore the political trends in the country. The British government had sent Sir Stafford Cripps and Lord Pethick Lawrence to formulate a plan acceptable to both the Congress and the Muslim League. Meetings were going on between these two groups and other political groups all over the country. We believed that the NCWI should not ignore these important events but rather present the women's point of view before the two British statesmen. Keeping this in mind, it was decided that Mrs. B.C. Dutt, a member of the executive committee, and I, as the Honorary General Secretary, would meet these British dignitaries. This was in April 1946. The NCWI had decided to support the stand taken by Congress.

The first Asian Relations Conference was called by our first Prime Minister, Jawaharlal Nehru, in 1947. It was the first time that various countries of this great continent got together on one platform to discuss their problems and formulate plans relevant to Asia only. I have always been impressed with how many cultures and languages are found in Asia. In comparison, Europe seems homogeneous. This conference marked the awakening of a continent and the realization that Asia had an important role to play in world affairs. It was like watching a giant awaken from a deep slumber.

While in Bombay I decided to study for my doctorate. I have always been fond of studying and fascinated by history so I decided to work toward a doctorate in Indian history. When I discussed this with my husband I found that he was keen to have me complete a doctorate in economics. I tried to explain that in my time the University of the Punjab did not allow women students to study economics, so I knew nothing about this subject. But he was very insistent and promised to tutor me. He even purchased a book on the elementary principles of economics. There was no time for lessons, though. After his office closed he went to the Willingdon Club to play bridge, and Sundays and holidays were taken up by races at the Race Club and playing bridge with friends. But to please him I made an appointment to meet with the university authorities in Bombay.

They were rightfully astonished at my request to be allowed to do a doctorate in economics when I knew next to nothing about the subject. When I explained how keen my husband was, these Indian gentlemen, intimately familiar with our family system, understood my request. They suggested that I study the subject intensively for a couple of years, pass the master's examination in economics, and then apply for admittance to the doctoral program.

Fortunately for me, a relation of ours, Prem Thapar, came to Bombay and stayed with us. When he saw me struggling with elementary economics, he asked what I was doing. Once he had heard the story, he took my husband to task. He thought it quite foolish for a history major to switch to a totally new subject like economics and begin preparing for the master's examination.

I heaved a sigh of relief and promptly went to meet the head of the History Department of St. Xavier's College, a Jesuit priest. After hearing about my political background the research topic he suggested was "Lord Dalhousie's Responsibility for the Indian Mutiny." I thoroughly approved of this idea and immediately set to work under his guidance. I had worked on this topic for about two years, and the research was almost complete, when the Reverend Father suggested that I go to Delhi for two months to consult records in the National Archives. This was in 1947.

That year, Congress and the Muslim League had reached a compromise, and an interim government had been formed with Jawaharlal Nehru as Prime Minister and Liaquat Ali Khan of the Muslim League as Finance Minister. C.H. Bhabha, a Parsi businessman from Bombay, became Minister of Energy. A good friend of ours, he was always pressing my husband to return to Delhi as Chair of the Delhi Central Electric Power Authority, the first nationalized undertaking in the country. I always protested that my husband was a chartered accountant not an electrical engineer. Actually I did not want to leave Bombay, where we had a comfortable life and were well settled. But Mr. Bhabha would not listen. His constant refrain was that the country needed officers like my husband. Finally my husband left the Income Tax Appellate Tribunal and returned to Delhi in July 1947 as the Chair of the Central Electric Power Authority.

Under these circumstances I needed to remain in Bombay to care for the children and pack our belongings. Even if I could have made some arrangements for the children, Delhi was in turmoil, and it would have been impossible to undertake a serious research project. Thousands of people were pouring across the newly constructed border every day. Everyone who could help was enlisted to assist in rehabilitating the refugees.

The children and I returned to Delhi late in November 1947. After settling down in our house on Alipur Road in old Delhi, I offered my services to the Ministry of Rehabilitation. My work there was to continue for almost seven years, and I never resumed my research at the National Archives. I carefully preserved my research notes for many years in hopes of completing my thesis now that I was in Delhi and could use records at the archives, but there were other demands on my time. A developing country like India needed volunteers willing to work among women and children. Although my welfare work superseded my pursuit of a higher degree, I feel I am richer for having had the opportunity to gain firsthand knowledge of the problems faced by my people.

11

With the Ministry of Rehabilitation, 1948–55

My husband was transferred back to Delhi in July 1947 as Chair of the Delhi Central Electric Power Authority—the first nationalized concern. He moved to Delhi alone, as our house at 32 Alipur Road was not yet ready for occupation. The children and I followed in November of the same year, so I missed the midnight ceremony* that declared India free and independent.

By this time, thousands of displaced women and children had made their way to Delhi and hundreds were en route. They had to be settled, and a Ministry of Rehabilitation was formed with K.C. Neogy as the first Minister in Charge. A Women's Section, under the leadership of Srimati Rameshwari Nehru, was set up to look after and develop schemes to rehabilitate the displaced women and children. Many of the experienced social workers joined in, including Mrs. Hannah Sen as Secretary and Mrs. Raksha Saran. As soon as we were settled I joined the Women's Section and spent my mornings at the headquarters. Most of my time was spent in the reception office listening to the heart-rending stories of the women who came to us for assistance.

---

*August 15, 1947.

Our son, Pradip, had already registered at the Doon School in Dehra Dun, but when the call came for him to join the school in January 1948 he was ill with a bad attack of dysentery and the doctors felt he should remain at home a while longer. In the meantime, he would attend school in New Delhi while the girls went to Presentation Convent near the main railway station. When the fuel shortage made it impossible for the school authorities to send their buses that great distance, I decided to remove the three of them from school and engaged a tutor to teach them at home. The tutor was a benign-looking Sikh gentleman and a great favorite of all my three children. My youngest, Saloni, was barely five years old and she was just learning the alphabet then. She used to slip a two-*anna* coin [small change] into the master's cloth bag and would not take the money back when he discovered it. He was greatly touched by this gesture.

By this time, the war with Pakistan over Kashmir had begun. A senior ICS officer and his wife, Sir Gurunath and Lady Bewoor, had lost their elder son, Madhav, in the Second World War. Lady Bewoor was especially keen to do something for *jawans* [soldiers], so she suggested that she and I and Madhav's wife serve tea, biscuits, and cigarettes to the passing troops at Auckinleck Aramghar at the Delhi Main Railway Station. Following her suggestion we began to do this every evening. During the day we collected donations of milk, sugar, biscuits, and cigarettes and were able to give each *jawan* a hot cup of tea with biscuits and two cigarettes when the trains passed through the main station. We carried this on for several months.

The army officers' wives had a club called Snowball Club, where they used to knit stockings and scarves for the *jawans* on the Kashmir border. The convalescent soldiers from the Military Hospital were entertained at teas given at the homes of these women. Although I had nothing to do with the defense forces, I was asked by my friend Lady Elizabeth Russell, wife of General Sir Dudley Russell, who had opted to remain with the Indian army, if I would entertain these *jawans* in my garden. I readily agreed and was told that the nurses accompanying them would bring board games to keep them occupied. All the hostess had to do was provide tea and food, but I wanted to do something else. Tea and snacks would be delivered from Maiden's Hotel so I did not have to bother with that. I discussed an entertainment program with my children's tutor, and he suggested that I hire a regular band from Lajpat Rai Market. This band gave the tea a cheerful atmosphere, and *jawans* ignored their games in favor of requesting their favorite tunes from Indian films.

The first break that I had after I started working with the Rehabilitation Ministry (or "attending P Block," as we referred to going to the office) came during the *Holi* festival in 1948. Mrs. Rameshwari Nehru, Mrs. Hannah Sen, and Mrs. Raksha Saran were all going out of town. The office was closed, but since a group of displaced women was expected I was left in charge. My residence telephone number had been given to Lady Mountbatten in case she needed to communicate with me. No one knew whether these women were Hindus or Muslims, but Mrs. Nehru had the impression that about a hundred Hindu women were expected. Arrangements had been made to take them to the Muslim Women's Transit Camp in Darya Ganj. Mrs. Nehru asked me to go to this camp and await their arrival, as it was not certain when they would reach Delhi. Right after breakfast I went to the Muslim Women's Transit Camp and met Miss Hill (Lady Mountbatten's private secretary) and Sri B.N. Banerjee, Secretary of the United Council for Relief and Welfare (an organization established by Lady Mountbatten to assist in relief work), who were touring the camp. They asked why I was there on a holiday and I told them of this group of women that we expected. Both Miss Hill and Mr. Banerjee felt that Hindu women should not spend even one night in the Muslim Women's Transit Camp and insisted that some other arrangement be made. I telephoned the Secretary of the Ministry of Rehabilitation, Sri S.K. Kripalani. He professed total ignorance of this problem. Finally I went to meet the Minister concerned, Sri Neogy, and placed the problem before him. He also felt that under no circumstances should the two groups—Hindus and Muslims—be accommodated together. He promptly sent for one of the undersecretaries of the Ministry, Sri R. Gautam, and ordered him to make alternate arrangements. Mrs. Suchinta Sethi, in charge of one block of the Working Women's Hostel on Curzon Road, was contacted and ordered to make arrangements for receiving this contingent. I went home with an easier mind, ate, and returned to the Muslim Women's Transit Camp. When I returned to the camp I was told by the superintendent that the group had arrived and was settling in. On being asked who signed the receipt, the superintendant said that she had, as the contingent was all Muslim women. Somehow Mrs. Nehru had been wrongly informed. When the office reopened after the holidays, I was recounting my experience with great zeal to Mrs. Saran when I was sent for by Mrs. Nehru. She was not at all happy that I had to approach the Minister himself to solve this problem.

The work of rehabilitation continued. Mrs. Nehru felt that since the need for rehabilitation had assumed great proportions, the work could not be confined to Delhi, and a Women's Section in the central ministry was imperative. So Mrs. Nehru took charge of the Central Women's Section and Mrs. Hannah Sen was also transferred there as its Secretary. Mrs. Matthai and I became joint directors of the Women's Section in Delhi. Things were beginning to settle down and we felt that it was necessary to train these refugee women to stand on their own feet. The number of training centers was increased to twenty-two, and a diploma course in tailoring and cutting was introduced. Most of the centers trained only women, but some trained men as well. We had a shop in Connaught Place, the heart of New Delhi, where items made in the training centers could be sold.

Besides these centers, the Women's Section ran a home for displaced widows and their children in two adjoining bungalows. Here the women were taught how to tailor and how to make dhurries. The small children lived with their mothers, but the older children were sent to school—the boys to Ram Bagh House and the girls to Satya Narain Home, both in *Subzi Mandi* [a section of old Delhi]. These were both residential schools, and we provided extra teaching and support staff. After some time, a separate residential school for girls in classes eight through ten was needed, so we started a third home in Mehrauli, on the outskirts of Delhi. The Women's Section was given a grant for all this work by the Ministry of Rehabilitation.

Another section, the Loan Section, was set up to assist displaced men, older students, senior citizens, and invalids. It was here that petty shopkeepers and deserving students could go to apply for loans. The former shopkeepers were given business loans, the students granted scholarships. Those who were ill were given twenty-five rupees per monnth for food and other necessities. For treatment they were referred to the TB Center at Irwin Hospital.

Several senior citizens who had lost all their property in Pakistan and were unable to start all over again in Delhi came to the Loan Section for financial assistance. Unfortunately, under the government scheme we could only give them a stipend of twenty-five rupees per month, which was never enough to provide them with food and shelter.

I remember an elderly man from Gujarat who had donated fifty thousand rupees to a hospital only a few months before Partition. He wept so much that Mr. Seth, the Rehabilitation Secretary for Delhi, asked me to take him away to P Block and give him the sanctioned stipend. The man pleaded for another twenty-five rupees in the name of his wife, but we were bound by the rules and could not be of any further assistance. Whenever he came to P Block to collect his stipend, I would give him a substantial meal and have him dropped home in my office car to save him his bus fare.

The Rehabilitation Ministry had started a Maintenance Allowance Scheme for the small property owners until such time as their claims were settled. I was a nominated member, along with Pandit Radhakishnan, Sri Ram Gulati, and other social workers. The ministry laid down a number of rules: the maximum amount allowed one person was a hundred rupees per month, the minimum ten. The amount of the stipend was to be decided depending on their property in Pakistan.

When Sri John Mathai, Finance Minister in the Government of India, resigned from his post in the middle of 1952 to return to his old post with Tatas,* Mrs. Mathai went with him. She resigned as Honorary Director of the Women's Section and I took her place. Because the Women's Section had expanded its work considerably, I suggested it be renamed to reflect this. The Delhi authorities agreed and it became the Social Welfare Rehabilitation Directorate.

The total annual budget of the Women's Section was about eight hundred thousand rupees. All the voluntary workers, like Mrs. Nehru, Mrs. Hannah Sen, Mrs. Mathai, Mrs. Saran, and myself, were given the sum of one rupee per month to conform with Government Servant Conduct Rules.

When I took over as Honorary Director, there was also a change in the central government. Sri Mohanlal Saxena had resigned as Minister of Rehabilitation, and Ajit Prasad Jain took his place. He and I took over our respective offices on the same day—June 1, 1952. For the first few days I took him to our various homes and training centers to acquaint him with the rehabilitation work going on in Delhi. This helped to develop a good working relationship between the two of us. The Working Women's Hostel on Curzon Road was confined to two buildings, each with a superintendent. We ran a community kitchen for

---

*One of India's major business organizations.

the women and provided for all their meals. According to the hostel rules they had to return home by 11:00 P.M. But our new Minister, Sri Jain, belonged to the old school and did not approve of the women staying out so late. In vain I tried to explain that they were working women, not university students. At first he insisted that they return to the hostel by 8:00 P.M., but I knew this would lead to a lot of opposition, so I bargained with him, and we eventually agreed to a 10:00 P.M. curfew. I exercised all my ingenuity and tact to persuade the women to obey these new rules. I am thankful to say that they cooperated wholeheartedly. I do not of course mean that all the women were amenable, and in those cases we had to take strict action. In those rare cases I would go personally to meet the woman who had failed to abide by the rules, and in some cases I would escort her to the home of her guardian.

I remember one case very well. I received a letter, in Hindi, from an Indian woman in England asking for accommodation in the hostel. As a reference she gave the name of the late Sri S.K. Upadhyaya, M.P., whose contact with the Nehru family began in 1923 when he worked as a private secretary to Motilal Nehru in Naini Tal. His loyalty to the family was unquestionable, and we all knew him very well. He told me that the woman, Pushpa, had been married before Partition. When they came to India her husband demanded five thousand rupees from Pushpa's father. But the poor man was unable to produce the cash, so the husband refused to take Pushpa back. She was trained as a telephone operator, got a job, and lived in our hostel. Some time later a young Indian living in the United Kingdom met Upadhyayaji and told him he wanted to get married to an Indian girl. Upadhyayaji knew of Pushpa's case, so with all good intentions, and without arranging a legal separation or divorce for Pupsha from her first husband, he persuaded Pushpa to marry the young man. When I asked if the bridegroom had produced his relations or any credentials Upadhyayaji replied in the negative. He took the couple to a Hindu temple, where they exchanged garlands and were declared married. Moreover, Upadhyayaji had persuaded Pushpa's father to part with five thousand rupees in dowry. The couple then left for the United Kingdom by ship. By the time the boat had reached Aden, the new husband had persuaded Pushpa to sign a paper saying that she was his sister. When the ship reached Dover, the young man disappeared with the cash, leaving Pushpa stranded in a strange country. Fortunately she had the good sense to contact our High Commissioner in London, Mr. Krishna Menon, who got her to London. This was when she contacted me. She had no job when she returned to Delhi. The minimum charge at our hostel was then fifty rupees per month. Mrs. Nehru paid Pushpa's hostel fees for three months until she found a job. Her rehabilitation was difficult because our traditions were strict. Pupsha flouted all the hostel's rules and regulations so that finally we had to ask her to leave.

Where she went after that I do not know. I feel that the second marriage, so thoughtlessly arranged by Upadhyayaji, swept away all her inhibitions. Before asking her to vacate the hostel, we had to have her treated for various diseases, which she had contracted through her free and easy ways with men.

Because the government was anxious to settle the displaced women and their children, they acquired a large plot of land in Lajpat *nagar*. This was developed as a displaced persons' colony, and one-room dwellings were constructed in rows where widows could live with their children. Homes such as Ram Bagh and Satya Narain, and the one in Mehrauli, were vacated and the buildings returned to their respective owners. The two bungalows used as widows' homes were temporarily handed over to the police. We moved out of the premises on a cold December day in 1952. Distributing rations to each family was a Herculean task that took two to three days to complete. In addition, each family had to be provided with cooking and eating utensils, fuel for cooking, a lantern, and some bedding. The women were thrilled when they understood that they could keep their children with them. Community kitchens were abolished, and families were permitted to cook and eat whatever they pleased.

There were still had a large number of parentless children for whom a separate children's home had been constructed in the same complex. We kept the boys' section separate from the girls' section, but there was a common kitchen. The school-age children attended the nearby municipal/government schools, while a primary school for toddlers was set up in the children's home. The American Women's Club donated a fully equipped children's park with swings and seesaws for the complex. The residential staff were provided with two-room quarters so they could be near at hand.

The formal opening of Kasturba *Niketan* [a building named after Gandhi's wife] was presided over by the President of India, Dr. Rajendra Prasad; the Children's Home was opened later by Prime

Minister Pandit Jawaharlal Nehru. Every morning all the children gathered at Kasturba Niketan for a free glass of milk, which they were to drink on the premises (many of the children wanted to save some of their milk for their mothers). Widows who were able to earn enough to support themselves were moved to Amar Colony. Finally, only the elderly women and those who could not care for themselves were left at Kasturba Niketan. The Children's Home continued, but no new children were admitted, and the resident children eventually moved out to start lives of their own. I was fortunate in being able to assist some of them in getting jobs with the Delhi administration. After I resigned from the Social Welfare and Rehabilitation Department in 1954, I lost touch with the home and its inmates.

Before I relinquished my post, the Ministry of Rehabilitation decided to rehabilitate the displaced widows who had not taken shelter in the homes but were living with friends and relatives. Most of them were able to earn a decent living, so we formed the *Bhartiya Mahila* [Indian Women's] Craft Society with myself as President. The government acquired a large tract of land across the river Jamuna where they could give each widow a one-room dwelling on twenty-five square yards of land. Seventy-five of these small houses were constructed in record time and handed over to these women, who could now live with their children. Since this was to be a women's colony in Gandhi Nagar, many thought that across the road a similar colony should be built to house entire families so women would feel safe. That scheme never materialized, but the Gandhi *Nagar Mahila* [Women's] Colony flourished. With the expansion of Delhi in all directions, the land in this colony has become very valuable.

The Ministry of Rehabilitation decided to open schools for displaced children which could provide industrial training as well as academic courses. A plot of land was acquired in Shahdara, a suburb of New Delhi, and I personally supervised the construction of a school for three hundred girls. Unfortunately, the idea of a vocational training institute for girls was at least a decade too early. What trades would be useful to them other then dyeing and printing fabrics and tailoring and stitching? So it was run like a normal school. The Delhi administration gave us a grant for 95 percent of the expenses; we had to raise the rest of the funds. I persuaded the Shahdara Municipal Committee to make up the deficit, but, as is usual in all government departments, the grants did not come in time and the funds necessary to run the school, for staff salaries, for example, had to be found. Shahdara was quite far away from my home, and I was responsibile for distributing salaries from the Girls' Fund and later on reimbursing this fund from the grant-in-aid. The government auditors criticized me for illegally using funds. In 1957 I finally persuaded the Delhi administration to take over the school. Now it is a proper girls' school, and the idea of vocational training has been dropped completely.

The last year I was the director of the Social Welfare and Rehabilitation Directorate, 1953–54, I was given an ad hoc grant of one hundred thousand rupees by the Delhi administration to distribute to petty shopkeepers who wanted to start businesses for rehabilitation. The grant had to be distributed by March 31 of that year and it was already January. Once I had accepted this additional grant, I realized what a tremendous task I had undertaken. We had a list of persons whom we had not been able to help earlier, but tracing them was difficult. If we found them, they had to bring two guarantors each and reapply. According to the rules, the grants were to range from one thousand to five thousand rupees per applicant. I could only manage to distribute these grants by keeping the office open until midnight or later. The assistant director of accounts, Sri Kailash Chandra, and the assistant director of the Loans Section, Sri D.C. Nanda, worked tirelessly to accomplish this distribution. I once phoned the Secretary of Rehabilitation, Sri Govind H. Seth, at 11:00 P.M. for a clarification of some point. He asked me if I had insomnia and was shocked when I told him that I was in the office and that the Accounts Department and Loans Department were also functioning. The corridors of P Block were teeming with people who had come to claim some portion of the rehabilitation grant. Mr. Seth was so upset by my late call that he closed his office on 5 Alipur Road (old Delhi) where he was also working late and drove all the way to P Block to personally supervise the work we were doing.

Since all the checks we distributed had to be cleared by March 31, I went personally to the agent of the Imperial Bank (now known as the State Bank of India) to solicit his support in this venture. Delhi had an assembly in those days, and I got hold of a Member of the Legislative Assembly, Sri Ganga Prasad, and asked him to sit at the bank all day long to guarantee my signature on the checks. While the task of distributing small amounts of money to poor refugees who wanted a chance to go on with their lives sounds simple, I know firsthand how difficult it is to accomplish. After his first visit, Mr. Govind Seth came over to our office practically every night until March 31, when we completed our work.

Another landmark in my term as Honorary Director was when I was asked by our Minister for Rehabilitation, Sri Ajit Prasad Jain, if I would take over part of the work of the Custodian of Evacuee Property. The Custodian had been so busy that those who were to receive allowances had not been paid for six months. The Minister was keen that payments be brought up to date. The Custodian of Evacuee Property was an eminent personality. I took over this work from Sri Naval Kishore. My budget jumped suddenly from nine hundred thousand to three million rupees, and I made it clear I would need the assistance of Sri Kailash Chandra and Sri D.C. Nanda, the men who had worked so closely with me in distributing small loans.

These two gentlemen and I started work on this scheme and paid off small allowances to persons as far as the allocated budget permitted. But to clean up the arrears and bring the payments up to date, we needed an extra hundred thousand rupees. I asked Sri M.L. Khanna, the Undersecretary in the Rehabilitation Ministry, to solve this problem, but he threw up his hands and pointed out that the ministry could not sanction such a large amount without going to the Prime Minister and Cabinet for approval. This would take at least six months. I thanked him and decided to try my luck with the Minister. I went to see him and made my request. At first he laughed at my request, but I reminded him that he was the one who wanted all the arrears to be cleared and payments brought up to date. He promised to send a check the next day. No one had even seen a check for such a large amount, and the entire staff trooped into my office to look at it. We were able to clear all the accounts, and my job was over.

During these years, I learned a great deal about the lives of ordinary people. I remember the case of a sixteen-year-old girl who had been married to a forty-five-year-old man in Jullundur. After her marriage she ran away from her in-laws' house and came to Delhi to be with some distant relations of her parents. She was not very certain of the address, though, so she wandered about the Delhi Main Railway Station. A Good Samaritan took care of her and helped her find her distant relatives' house. It so happened that the lady of the house was away, but when the son of the house saw a lone young girl seeking shelter he tried to molest her. She ran away and by evening was at the clock tower in Chandni Chowk. As a crowd collected around her, she became like a hunted animal surrounded by beasts. A Punjabi woman who was passing by inquired what the trouble was, and hearing that a young girl was being harassed she shouted that a girl was missing from her street. The crowd parted, and she took the girl by the hand and pulled her out of the crowd. She then took her to the nearest police station. Our school in Satya Narain House was still running, so the police sent for the superintendent, Raj Dulari, and handed the girl over to her for safe custody. The next day Raj Dulari brought the girl to the office and I sent her to the Women's Home until we could make the necessary inquiries. Her in-laws came and showed me her wedding photograph. The husband also came, but he did not look normal to me and I was very upset with the family for this misalliance. The girl refused to go back to her in-laws until her father came to the home. Her father confessed that he had sold the girl to that family for five hundred rupees. After some months the girl went back to her husband. To her it must have seemed the best option available.

There was another case of two widowers, both laborers, who had daughters and lived next door to each other in old Delhi. One fine morning they decided to exchange their daughters in marriage. Both men were quite old, and the girls were young. One of the girls accepted her husband but the other was only sixteen years old. She could not get used to her marriage, and, because she was very pretty, her husband locked her up in a room each morning when he went out to work. One day she ran away from the house and was found wandering in the Qutab Minar at dusk. She did not seem normal, and someone brought her to our school in Mehrauli. The girl stayed with us for several months until she regained her mental balance. Her husband traced her to the school in Mehrauli and came to visit her and beg her to return to him. The staff tried to tell her that her place was with her husband. Finally the man came to my office and said that he had been allotted some land in the Punjab and would be able to keep his wife in comfort. I scolded him for his brutal behavior and told him that I would not permit the girl to go back with him. But the staff persuaded the girl to return with him to his newly acquired farm.

12

General Elections, 1952, 1957, and 1971

India held its first general elections in 1952. As I had been a political activist in the Punjab, I decided I would like to be a candidate for Parliament for the constituency of Ambala/Kalka/Simla. I paid the requisite candidate's fees and went to see Sri Rafi Ahmed Kidwai, a member of the Parliamentary Board, to find out the attitude of members. Sri Kidwai used to live in Western Court and I knew him personally since he too belonged to Uttar Pradesh. As soon as he saw me he said the Parliamentary Board had accepted my name for the constituency.

When I came home I reported this to my husband. He was very pleased, and the two of us waited for a letter to confirm the board's decision. But we heard nothing from the Congress office or from anywhere else. Finally we decided to go to the Congress office to see what had happened. The staff there said that my name had been on the accepted list of candidates until about 3:00 P.M., but then the Prime Minister received a telegram from Lala Duni Chand Ambalvi (this name was added because he resided in Ambala) saying that this seat should be allotted to his son Sri Tek Chand. The committee members looked to Jawaharlal Nehru for guidance. He said, "since she is my niece I won't interfere," and he refused to vote either way. The committee assumed this meant he was indifferent as to who the candidate would be, so my name was scratched out and that of Tek Chand substituted.

Ajit Prasad Jain, the Rehabilitation Minister, who had been out on tour, returned and was greatly concerned at this turn of events. He took me to meet Sri Govind Vallabh Pant, Chief Minister of Uttar Pradesh and a well-respected All-India leader. Pantji said he would try and accommodate me in Uttar Pradesh, but my experience in Congress work in that region was nil. Another possibility was to run for the New Delhi seat, but that was also complicated. Mrs. Sucheta Kripalani and her husband Acharya J.B. Kripalani had broken away from Congress and formed a separate group known as *Kisan Mazdoor Praja* [Peasants and Workers party]. Mrs. Kripalani was contesting the Delhi seat on behalf of her party. When Sri Jain took me to meet Rafi Ahmed Kidwai again, we were told that although Mrs. Kripalani was no longer in Congress they had decided not to oppose her because of her past record and that of her husband.

Meanwhile, one of the Congress leaders of Delhi, Sri Desh Bandhu Gupta, had died. Delhi was to become a state with a legislature and a cabinet, and Sri Gupta had been hoping to become the first Chief Minister of Delhi. His sudden death left a void. Chaudhury Brahm Prakash was also aspiring to be Chief Minister and did not want to oppose Mrs. Kripalani by putting up a strong candidate. So my name was suggested, and the Prime Minister was told that I would get barely three thousand votes and would probably lose my deposit. But the scheme fulfilled the Delhi Congress Committee's desire to run a candidate for New Delhi.

Sri Mehr Chand Khanna, adviser in the Ministry of Rehabilitation, was a close friend of my husband's. He telephoned me every morning to discourage me from accepting the Congress nomination. I got fed up and told my husband that I was going to write to Chandhury Brahm Prakash, President of the Delhi Congress Committee, asking him to withdraw my name. My husband advised me to go to my office (I was still director of the Social Welfare and Rehabilitation Directorate) and suggested that we discuss it later that evening. But that evening we received the news that my name had been accepted by the Parliamentary Board as a Congress nominee for the New Delhi constituency. I decided to run. All this was ironic, because Sucheta Kripalani and I had been classmates at Kinnaird College in Lahore.

My mother came from Allahabad to help in the campaign. Between my work with the people from the Punjab and my work in the Ministry of Rehabilitation, I was not the unknown figure the Delhi Congress had assumed. But I had a tough time organizing supporters and running my campaign. It seemed as though Congress leaders were determined to help Mrs. Kripalani at every turn. If I brought the grievances of the refugees to the appropriate authorities, these same people would visit the area with me, promise to have the grievances redressed, and then return to the office and telephone Mrs. Kripalani and suggest she visit that particular area. Then she could take the credit for getting the refugees' grievances redressed.

For a long time I did not know this was happening. I used to wonder why she and I were visiting the same localities. When I found out, I asked Chaudhury Brahm Prakash to do something to stop this sabotage. He would solemnly promise to take action, but things went on as before. Finally I telephoned Sri Lal Bahadur Shastri, General Secretary of the All-India Congress Committee, and went to see him. I told him what was happening and that I was going to lose the seat unless the central office appointed someone to be in charge of the New Delhi constituency who was not biased and would supervise my election campaign. He expressed great concern but said that the President, meaning Jawaharlal Nehru, was touring the South and that he would await his return before doing anything. Of course, that was also an eyewash.

The long and the short of it was that I received more than forty thousand votes, but Mrs. Kripalani received about five or six thousand more; I do not remember the exact figures. At one point in the counting she considered conceding to me, but her workers persuaded her to wait and see. And in the end they were right.

There were eleven Assembly seats in the New Delhi constituency. Congress lost the parliamentary seat and one Assembly seat. I went personally to President Jawaharlal Nehru and asked him to explain this, as all those who voted for the Assembly candidates would automatically vote for the parliamentary candidate. He asked me to send a written report, which I did, laying the blame for my defeat squarely on Sri Mehr Chand Khanna and Chaudhury Brahm Prakash. Being honest and straightforward does not pay in our country, and certainly not with Chaudhury Brahm Prakash, who never forgave me. My husband was so upset at Sri Khanna's perfidy that he broke off his long friendship, and though they reconciled many years later, things were never the same between them.

Meanwhile all candidates got circulars from the Congress office to carefully watch their opponents' accounts. At a reception given to Sri Asaf Ali, our ambassador to Switzerland, there was a lot of talk about the returns filed by Mrs. Kripalani for her election campaign, suggesting they did not conform to the norms laid down by the Election Commission. I was asked what I was going to do about it as this could be the basis of an election petition. My reply was that I would go home, consult my husband, and try to find out if there were any truth to these rumors.

It transpired that Mrs. Kripalani had filed two separate returns. The first one went against the orders of the Election Commission, which officially permitted only six paid workers; she had listed a large number. She was ill in the hospital when this mistake was brought to her notice, but before the amended document was filed people began to talk. Filing a second, amended return was also against the rules, but the election commissioner, who was from the same state as Mrs. Kripalani, allowed her to do so. My husband was a lawyer as well as a chartered accountant, so he personally drafted my election petition and I filed an appeal against the election of Mrs. Kripalani. It created a furor. Sri Gopal Swaroop Pathak (later Vice-President of India) was a friend of the family, and he sent a message that he would fight the case on my behalf.

There was pressure on me to withdraw my petition. Even Maulana Azad called and said that if I did not withdraw my petition I would never be considered for any election in the future. I reported that I was going to win my petition but that if the Congress High Command favored Mrs. Kripalani despite her position with the opposition, I would not approach them in the future for any favors.

Sri Ajit Prasad Jain went through my petition very carefully and was firmly convinced that I would win, an opinion shared by everyone who brought the question up in his presence. He also warned me that several members of the Congress High Command would pressure me, in the President's name, to withdraw my petition. He advised me to reply that I would like the President to make this request directly to me. Under no circumstances should I listen to secondhand reports. It all turned out as he predicted. I was approached by Sri Lal Bahadur Shastri and asked to withdraw my petition. I said I would do so only if the President asked me to do so. He then invited me to meet with him in Teen Murti House, the residence of the Prime Minister. We sat on the back lawns discussing the issue, and when he had assured himself that I would withdraw it on the conditions already known to him, he said he would go and talk with Jawaharlal in his office. I waited and waited, but Shastriji never returned, so I went home. A month or so later I met Shastri—he was then Railway Minister, and I was the Chair of the Northern Railway Employees' Union—and asked him why he had left me sitting alone like that. He replied that he had gone upstairs and spoken to the Prime Minister. Jawaharlal had told him that I was well within my rights to file a petition and that he would not interfere.

The petition dragged on, as such petitions usually do, for four and a half years. Some constitutional point was referred to the Supreme Court of India and then Chief Justice of India Sri Mehr Chand Mahajan assured me personally that it would be taken up after the summer vacation. Meanwhile, Sri Mahajan retired. The new Chief Justice, Sri B.K. Mukerjee, was unaware of his predecessor's commitment to me. After the vacation was over, we waited and waited, but there was no sign of my petition being addressed. So I wrote a personal letter to the Chief Justice. My husband was horrified and said I would be cited for contempt of court. Instead, Chief Justice Mukerjee replied that my documents had not yet been received from the Punjab High Court. Anyway, this made things much clearer. The documents were finally sent from Chandigarh and the point decided in my favor. Then the three-member tribunal appointed to hear the petition started its work. It was the most confused judgment that I have ever read, but of course I am not a lawyer. The judgment first condemned me for my acts of omission and commission, then condemned Mrs. Kripalani, accepted my petition, withdrew the seat from Mrs. Kripalani, and declared it a vacant seat. The tribunal did not allot the seat to me. By this time it was April 1956 and I had gone to New York at the invitation of the Committee of Correspondence, an affiliate of the National Council of Women of the United States, to attend a seminar on the role of women in the community.

In New York I received a cable from my husband that I had won my election petition. I immediately wrote to Mrs. Gandhi that I was in the United States and from there would go to Great Britain and Europe. However, if the Congress were planning a by-election in the near future I would return home. She replied that since the general elections of 1957 were more or less around the corner, Congress was not planning a by-election. She also mentioned that she was being persuaded to contest from New Delhi. I followed my original itinerary, completed my visits to various places in the United States and Canada, and landed in London in July 1956. My husband had taken one month's leave, so he was able to meet me there. We spent a few days in London and then went to mainland Europe, where we visited France, Germany, Switzerland, and Italy. It was my first visit abroad, and I enjoyed it very much.

When we returned to Delhi we encountered a lot of speculation regarding the forthcoming general elections. This time, Prime Minister Jawaharlal Nehru had decided not to give his opinions and deferred to the man he had appointed President of the All-India Congress Committee, Sri U.N. Dhebar.

In the five years from 1952 to 1957 I had done a lot of work with organizations designed to help children and laborers. I was Working President of the Northern Railway Employees' Union and President of the Lower Division Clerks' Union in the Ministry of Defense, the Fishermen's Union, and the Central Public Works Department Employees' Union with all its subsidiary branches. I was also President of the Union of Auto-Rickshas. Because of these offices I was very well known and decided to advance my claim for the parliamentary seat from New Delhi.

When the time came to decide who would be candidates for New Delhi, Sri Dhebar was in a dilemma. Unknown to his colleagues, he had already promised the New Delhi seat to Mrs. Sucheta Kripalani after persuading her to resign from the *Kisan Mazdoor Praja* party and rejoin the Congress. Once again the choice was between Mrs. Kripalani and me. As I mentioned earlier, the Prime Minister was not intervening in the work of the Congress Parliamentary Board, and, at any rate, he was on tour. When he returned he was asked by the Parliamentary Board to attend one meeting since there was some difficulty in choosing candidates from the Punjab. The Prime Minister agreed, but when he came to the meeting the question of the New Delhi parliamentary seat was taken up instead. Dhebar Bhai (as he was generally known) put forward his suggestion of nominating Mrs. Kripalani. Maulana Azad and Sri Lal Bahadur pressed my claim. It is reported that Maulana Azad went as far as saying that when I filed my election petition, he had called me to his house and personally requested that I withdraw my petition and that I had replied that I had a very strong case and I could win. He also related that he had threatened that if I refused him he would see that I was never again selected for any seat as a Congress nominee. In his view, since I had won my election petition, I was the natural candidate, and, if Sri Dhebar wanted to accommodate Mrs. Kripalani, she could very well be considered for any seat from Utter Pradesh since she had lived there for many years. Jawaharlal Nehru sat quietly throughout the discussion. Then Sri Dhebar said that he had already promised the seat to Mrs. Kripalani and as President of the Congress his word should be honored. It is said that Maulana Azad became so incensed at this injustice to an old Congress worker that he threw down his file and walked away from the meeting wondering why it had been called.

The decision was finally made that Mrs. Kripalani would run from the New Delhi seat. All night long I got telephone calls from various friends and well wishers asking me how I had offended Congress High Command. I telephoned Mr. M.O. Mathai at the Prime Minister's home the next morning and asked him to schedule an urgent appointment for me with the Prime Minister. He tried very diplomatically to ward me off, mentioning that since the case had already been decided there was no point in my meeting the Prime Minister. But as I was adamant, he asked me to come at lunchtime. I do not remember where Mrs. Gandhi was on that day, but Jawaharlal was lunching alone. When I met him I was very upset and with tears in my eyes asked him how he could tolerate such an injustice to me. I reminded him that in the 1952 election three Congresswomen had lost and two of them had been compensated with other appointments. Mrs. Durgabai Deshmukh was nominated as a member of the Planning Commission and later on became Chair of the newly constituted Central Social Welfare Board. Mrs. Renuka Ray was nominated a member of the West Bengal government. "Jawahar Bhai," I asked, "what about me? I never came to you with any request but since you were advocating social work, I devoted myself to welfare work all these years." He gave me a long lecture about how sincere work always brought its own reward and that I should not be disheartened.

I was hurt and upset by this injustice and announced that I would file my nomination as an Independent candidate. Mrs. Subhadra Joshi, President of the Delhi Congress Committee, promptly called an emergency meeting and expelled me from the Congress for six years. Undeterred, I carried on with a lot of support from the general public because I had worked among the common people and they felt that I had been done an injustice. Since then I have not renewed my membership of the Congress, though I still feel a sense of allegiance to that august body.

By this time Mrs. Kripalani was having a difficult time in her campaign. Her offices were demolished by the public, and she found it difficult to hold small meetings. She naturally complained to the Congress President. He called me to his office several times asking me to withdraw my name. I asked him why he was supporting Mrs. Kripalani. He replied that he was hoping to bring her husband Acharya Kripalani back into the Congress fold and thus lessen the opposition. I pointed out that Kripalaniji was still as vehemently opposed to the Congress as he was earlier. When I asked why Kripalani was so important, he replied that Kripalani had joined Congress as early as 1918. I informed him that my mother, Lado Rani Zutshi, was already a member of the Congress in 1918. He replied that he had never heard of my mother. I replied that since he was not in the Congress then, how could he have? Mrs. Kripalani herself joined the Congress after her marriage to Acharyaji in 1936—while I had already been to prison three times. And my mother and my two sisters, Janak and Shyama, had also actively participated in the freedom struggle and been imprisoned. Finally he asked me to come to his home in Kingsway Camp. He was living in the *harijan* colony. When I got there, he said, "Sister, why do you keep harping on this Parliament issue?" In return I asked, "Were you not the Chief Minister of Saurashtra and are you not now President of the All-India Congress?" He answered yes. Then I asked, "Dhebar Bhai, you make me the President of the Congress and I will forget all about Parliament." What could he say? Others told me that he said that I did not give him due respect as President of Congress.

This encounter left me feeling that my claim to the New Delhi seat in Parliament was quite justified. My good friend Rajkumari Amrit Kaur, Minister of Health in the Central Government, had also been denied nomination. As a loyal Congress worker she tried to persuade me to withdraw. I replied, "Rajkumarji, you will be elected to the Rajya Sabha. If you can guarantee me a seat in the Upper House, then I will withdraw." This went on for several days. Sucheta Kripalani was becoming unnerved as she felt she was facing a hostile public. When Jawaharlal Nehru returned from tour, he was expressly asked to intervene and have me withdraw from the election. The Congress was not getting good reports from the Uttar Pradesh, the Punjab, and Rajasthan, as there was a lot of sympathy for me there. Jawaharlal had no option but to call me to his residence. He used the sentimental, family approach with me since he was the head of our extended family. He told me he did not relish the idea of my sitting outside the Congress fold in Parliament if I did win. I brought to his attention the fact that I had been thrown out of the party. But he was very persuasive, and in the end I said I would consult my workers, who were waiting for me at home. The consensus was that since the Prime Minister had personally requested my withdrawal I had no option. My workers believed that the Prime Minister was a fair-minded person who would try to accommodate me elsewhere in some other capacity. I withdrew, but as it turned out, the hope that I would be accomodated elsewhere was a false one.

At the time of the United Nations General Assembly Session in 1957, some friends suggested that I could go as a member of the Indian delegation if the Prime Minister agreed. They would put in a word for me with Sri Krishna Menon, our Defense Minister and leader of the Indian Delegation. At the time the newspapers had been speculating about women members of Parliament as likely delegates. I went to see Jawaharlal and he suggested I ignore these accounts. He also said that the government was probably not going to include any women in the delegation as an austerity measure. This shocked me and I reacted by asking why it was a woman who would be sacrificed at the altar of austerity? When the delegates were nominated, I found the name of Mrs. Tarkeshwari Sinha included on the list. I promptly wrote a letter of protest to the Prime Minister, reminding him of his earlier conversations with me that no woman would be sent this time. Of course he replied that it had not been his decision.

Looking back at all the incidents, large and small, I find that, although we do belong to the Nehru family, but do not carry the name Nehru, we seem to lose politically. The services of my family to the nation during the independence struggle had been significant, but after India became free we were ignored. In 1957 my mother's name had been recommended by the Punjab Provincial Congress Committee for the Punjab Assembly. Lala Duni Chand Ambalvi put forward the name of his wife as a candidate. When the list was sent to Jawaharlal Nehru for final approval, he scratched out my mother's name and substituted that of Mrs. Duni Chand Ambalvi. Neither Mother nor I was ever given preference for a public position despite our long records of service to Congress. When Indira Gandhi became Prime Minister she was affectionate and friendly toward both of us, but that was all. Rajiv Gandhi followed in the footsteps of his mother and grandfather and showed no favoritism to our branch of the family.

13

Welfare Work after Partition

After I resigned from the Ministry of Rehabilitation, my welfare work among the general public increased fourfold. I was elected Chair of the Northern Railway Employees' Union and was constantly engaged in discussing the problems of the employees with higher authorities. This meant frequent trips to the office of the General Manager of the Northern Railways, Sardar Karnail Singh, a good friend of my husband's. Every time I entered his office he would jokingly remark, "My boss has come."

I was also a member of the Catering Advisory Committee for the Northern Eastern Railway. This required me to attend meetings outside of Delhi, and I once had to travel to Siliguri. Traveling all that distance alone when there were very few women travelers in the separate women's compartment was quite unpleasant, so I approached the Railway Minister, Sri Sham Nath, and asked to be transferred to the Catering Advisory Committee of the Northern Railway. The meetings of this Committee were held in New Delhi, and when the whole committee went on a conducted tour to check the food supplies at various stations, the farthest destination was Lucknow. I also visited the main railway station in Delhi to see for myself how food was prepared and distributed and to check on the vendors selling tea and snacks to railway passengers. I discovered that coffee was sold as tea by some vendors. When complaints were made about the bitter taste, the customers were informed that the fault lay in their palates. Often skim milk was sold as whole milk, but it was difficult to catch the sellers. If one called the railway police, the vendors would quickly move outside the station gates where the railway police had no jurisdiction. If one then approached the civil police, the vendors would step inside the railway compound. It was only with great difficulty that they were apprehended.

As I have always been interested in labor, I became the President of the Fishermen's Union, the Auto-Ricksha Union, and the Union of the Lower Division of Clerks in the Ministry of Defense. I was also the All-India President of the CPWD Employees' Union and its subsidiaries. No two unions had similar programs or similar demands so each unit needed special attention.

I was very keen that the men belonging to these various unions organize their womenfolk to tackle a range of important issues. With a little training, the women could look after problems such as school admission, sanitation, and health care. But whenever I raised the point the men would remark, "*Behanji* [elder sister], let us first get this demand settled and then we will organize our womenfolk." Of course, the right time never came because there was no end to the demands. This was a golden opportunity to bring women into the mainstream of the country's progress and it was lost. I believe the unions could have done far more for adult literacy and other nation-building programs.

I had a group of very dedicated young men who were very helpful in tackling other problems. This small group called themselves the *Swastheya* [Health] Committee. Our major work was to visit various areas in Delhi to see if the garbage and refuse were properly collected.

There was an area near Rohtak Road in old Delhi called Bagh Kare Khan. People had constructed unauthorized houses in this locality so the Municipal Committee of Delhi had no obligation to provide services. When we visited Bagh Kare Khan we found pools of dark, filthy water, unswept lanes, and no surfaced paths. Our first task was to tackle the lanes, and we laid bricks to make them look cleaner. Then I brought Rajkumari Amrit Kaur, the Minister of Health, Dr. Sushila Nayar, the Minister of Health for Delhi State, and Lala Sham Nath, who was then President of the Delhi Municipal Committee to see for themselves how a section of the people were living. The result: prompt action. Truckloads of earth were brought to fill the filthy pools and finally some amenities were provided. This area of Bagh Kare Khan is now Gulabi Bagh.

Besides my work with organized labor, I was involved with other groups. Some projects I started myself, for example, the milk-distributing center in a displaced persons camp at Purana Pila, the powdered milk for which I got from CARE. One of my workers, Indar Lal Bagga (a railway employee), was in charge. He organized the center very efficiently. Each child was given a card similar to a ration card, with dates to mark the milk consumed. Later on we developed a small child-care center by adding a few indoor games and some books. The center continued for as long as the camp was there. It closed down as the displaced families were allotted permanent accommodations in the different colonies being developed by the Ministry of Rehabilitation.

There was at one time a big labor camp on Rouse Avenue (now known as Deen Dayal Upadhyaya Marg). It was being supervised by Bindi Ram on my behalf, but all major decisions were taken by me. Bindi Ram was an employee of the Government of India Press on Rouse Avenue and had been allotted quarters nearby. This camp soon became my major project. I persuaded the people of the camp to have proper latrines and engage two sweepers for which each family paid twenty-five *paisa* every month. There was no bathing place for the women, so I asked the New Delhi Municipal Committee to put up a couple of water taps on the side wall of one of these hutments. We then put up a curtain to give the women some privacy. This camp continued in the same place for some years, but since the authorities had plans to develop this area the laborers had to move. The question then arose: Where would they go? The camp was large, consisting of more than fifty families. I approached our late Prime Minister Lal Bahadur Shastri, who was then the Minister for Railways. Beyond Tilak Bridge there was a vast piece of land belonging to the railways which was being used as a garbage dump. I requested that Shastriji allot that land to me free of charge for these laborers, and I promised to vacate it whenever the railways needed it. I then moved these families to that site but located them near the river Jumna so that they could not easily be seen.

A group of municipal employees, mostly in class 4,* had been given accommodations in Vinoba Puri Lajpat Nagar. When I started work

---

*The lowest class of employees; in this case, most of them were *harijans*.

among them I discovered that each family was heavily in debt. They had a very complicated system of calculating the interest. If they failed to pay the first installment of interest, the rate was doubled and quadrupled. Before long the amount first borrowed got lost in the interest due. Some had paid off the loan, yet with this system of interest they still remained deeply in debt. I called a meeting of these *harijans* and their creditors. After some discussion, both groups agreed to abide by my decision. I worked out each amount myself, calculating how much was originally borrowed and how much had been paid off. I discovered that on payday the creditors went to the office of the New Delhi Municipal Committee to snatch the pay from anyone who had a loan. With all their salary gone to pay of debts, these poor people had no option but to again borrow to meet their monthly expenditures. It had become a sort of vicious circle.

In my meeting with them, I announced that I would send one of my workers, J.S. Dara, to the New Delhi Municipal Committee on payday to collect all the pay packets and return to my house at Ashoka Road with them. We would then meet with all the creditors. I had earlier explained to the creditors that each *harijan* would pay the minimum amount of interest toward his loan and take the rest of the salary home for the use of his family. No creditor would get the exorbitant interest rates they had been receiving.

It took a lot of accounting to work this out, and it was only accomplished through the voluntary assistance of D.C. Nanda, who had been the Assistant Director in charge of loans when I was the Honorary Director in the Social Welfare and Rehabilitation Directorate. He would come over in the evening, sort out the accounts, and give ten rupees to the creditors, ten rupees for savings funds if the individual so desired, and the remainder to the individual employee. This system worked very well for many months. Within that time a few men were able to pay off their original loans with a reasonable amount of interest.

As the news of what we were doing spread among the lower ranks of the central government employees, I was besieged by requests to work out more or less the same system for other groups. The accounts got so complicated that I felt the need for a full-time paid accountant. I wrote to Prime Minister Jawaharlal Nehru, explaining my work among the *harijans* and the steps we were taking to relieve them of their indebtedness. I also sent a typed copy of the account of each person. To my dismay he replied that he had forwarded my papers to the Delhi

Bharat Sewak Samaj [Indian Service Society], which would henceforth look after the *harijans*. That organization was not interested in the way I was working, nor would their members take such pains with these people. My project had been passed on and I lost touch with the people I was helping.

In the first general elections, Sucheta Kripalani had won the New Delhi parliamentary seat. I am not sure she realized it, but the New Delhi Municipal Committee was divided into two groups. One sided with Sucheta Kripalani and the other with me. A large number of displaced persons had built small shacks on Humayun Road where they were engaged in small business to earn a living. When Prithivi Raj Market was constructed, the group supporting Sucheta Kripalani was immediately allotted shops, while the rest were deliberately left high and dry. In those days the New Delhi Municipal Committee was under the direct charge of the Deputy Commissioner of Delhi. I do not remember how many times I went to meet this Deputy Commissioner to ask him for an amicable settlement of the problem, but nothing happened. These shopkeepers were genuine displaced persons, so they were entitled to be allotted shops in the newly constructed Prithivi Raj Market. He would make some excuse or other, and although the shops were left vacant, they were not allotted to the squatters on Humayun Road.

Our Chief Commissioner (we did not have a Lieutenant Governor in those days) was an ICS officer, A.D. Pandit. He was an upright and conscientious officer. The two nominated Vice-Presidents on the New Delhi Municipal Committee were Bhai Mohan Singh and Begum Qudsia Zaidi. I discussed this problem with them. It was decided that they would go and meet with the Chief Commissioner accompanied by J.S. Dara and myself. We took all the relevant files from the New Delhi Municipal Committee and laid the problem squarely in front of the Chief Commissioner. He immediately asked the Deputy Commissioner to join the meeting. When the Deputy Commissioner saw me there, he claimed to have already decided to allot the shops and could not understand what the problem was. I retaliated that for the past five months I had done nothing but request this. Finally the Chief Commissioner ordered that Humayun Road squatters be allotted shops in Prithivi Raj Market, and eventually it was done.

On another occasion, four squatters who lived in the little by-lane leading from Man Singh Road to the roundabout, where the *Bharatiya*

Vidya Bhavan [Indian Educational Institution] is situated, sold tea and snacks to government officers in their offices to earn a living. When they heard that the New Delhi Municipal Committee was about to demolish their shacks, they immediately came to me. I went with them and stood under one of those huts, demanding to see the demolition order. Of course the municipal authorities did not have one, so they returned to their offices and complained about me. Meanwhile, I went home and contacted someone on the Municipal Committee. He assured me that most probably I was mistaken. Because these people were selling food, the health staff had gone there to check. He assured me that no action would be taken against these four squatters until they had been given regular shops. This was repeated again and again. Imagine my shock and surprise when I returned home for lunch the next day and found all four of these men, looking very upset, standing in front of my verandah. When I questioned them, they replied that their huts had been demolished. Not a stone or piece of wood remained intact. I was almost in tears when I saw what had happened. When I contacted the same gentleman on the Municipal Committee he was equally upset. So I insisted that the New Delhi Municipal Committee allot four shops to them that very day to rehabilitate them. It was done and they finally got settled.

In the early days following Independence we were not self-sufficient in food grains and we had to depend on other countries. Buying food grains was a drain on foreign exchange, so many of us tried to think of food substitutes. Sri K.M. Munshi, the Minister for Food and Agriculture, asked his wife, Lilavati Munshi, if she could organize the women to save rice and wheat. This was how the All-India Women's Central Food Council came into being. I was one of the Vice-Presidents and was active in running the Annapurna [goddess of food] Cafeteria in Delhi. Initially no rice or wheat was served. Members experimented with other food grains and alternative menus. I revived our grandmother's recipe for *singhara atta* [flour made from nuts grown in water] that was served on auspicious occasions. We also introduced South Indian dishes. The food was freshly cooked, neatly served, and reasonably priced, and so the Annapurna became an instant success. Soon other Annapurna cafeterias were started in other regions of the country, and several offices asked our help in organizing low-priced cafeterias.

The Food Council later on felt that the country needed trained personnel to run the hotels and restaurants. To provide this training, the College of Catering was set up under the auspices of the Food Council. The college was located on the premises of the *Bharatiya Vidya Bhavan* in Andheri, a suburb of Bombay. It offered a three-year diploma course. It was sometime after this that the Government of India and others became interested in setting up hotel management schools.

After some years, Mrs. Munshi closed down the Annapurna Cafeteria in Delhi. Although I was Vice-President, I felt that the Food Council had not really inspired people to experiment with grains other than rice and wheat. After Annapurna closed I took over the premises, with the permission of the Ministry of Housing, and started an organization called the Committee to Change Food Habits. We called our new cafeteria Rasika. The model was similar, but we introduced eggs and fish and concentrated on attracting women's groups. For housewives we organized cooking demonstrations in various locations throughout Delhi. After an intensive seven-day course, we encouraged the trainees to participate in a cooked food exhibition of noncereal dishes. The judges were housewives, as were the exhibitors, and prizes were given for the best three dishes. We held cooking demonstrations in various women's clubs and the defense personnel requested that we conduct these demonstrations for the army, navy, and air force women as well. We also gave a lunch in honor of the then Food Minister, inviting about a hundred guests to dine on noncereal dishes. Branching out from Delhi, we organized demonstrations in Bhopal, Madhya Pradesh, and Lucknow, Uttar Pradesh. By this time we had collected more than three hundred soybean recipes and were ready to have a cookbook published. Suddenly the Directorate of Estates in the Ministry of Works and Housing, our landlord, swooped down on us and took away our files, furniture, and equipment. Among the material never returned to us were the recipes we had so painstakingly collected.

There was a slight rise in the price of vegetables, and this became a women's issue. I called a meeting in sector 1 in Rama Krishna Puram, a government servants' colony of lower-rank officers belonging to various ministries. About two hundred women attended. After some discussion it was agreed that, with the assistance of their menfolk, the women could take charge of the selling of vegetables in their colony. About twenty women came forward offering by turns to look after the vegetable stall, keep accounts, and so forth. The menfolk also joined in. The men went to the wholesale vegetable market early in the morning and bought in bulk whatever was needed. They handed over their purchases to the women, who sold each item according to the demands of their customers. Meticulous accounts were kept. The women were free by 8:00 A.M. to attend to household duties. As word got around, a sweet seller also joined them, promising to keep his profits as low as possible. This idea was not only welcomed by all the residents, but it inspired the men to sell eggs, fish, bread, and other foodstuffs in small stalls after office hours. I also visited the evening stall. I am certain this project resulted in substantial savings; otherwise, the men and women would not have continued as long as they did. They were keen to make it permanent venture and requested that I get them permanent accomodations. I asked Mehar Chand Khanna, Minister for Housing, if he would be kind enough to allot one room to us for use as a small shop. He professed his inability to do so, and gradually the enthusiasm died out. The residents went back to their old habits of purchasing vegetables from hawkers.

One day while I was sitting in my office of the All-India Women's Central Food Council, Amar Kaur, sister of Bhagat Singh, came to see me. She had a very specific and important job she wanted me to do. It appeared that some years previously three young Sikhs had been implicated in a murder somewhere in the Punjab. They were found guilty and their appeal was ultimately rejected by the Supreme Court of India. Their petition for mercy had been rejected by the President of India. They were lodged in Ferozepur Jail, and the date of their execution had been fixed. Amar Kaur brought the astounding news that after all this time the real culprits had had a change of heart, had confessed to the crime, and were in police custody. When she spoke with me, there were only forty-eight hours remaining until the time of execution. I telephoned the Home Minister, Jai Sukhlal Hathi, and asked him to try to postpone the execution until all the necessary inquiries could be made. I pointed out to him that the condemned young men need not be released until he had all the details. By God's good grace, Jai Sukhlal Hathi accepted my suggestion, and the lives of these three young men were saved.

I think it must have been 1973 when I joined the National Federation of Indian Women. My special interest has been assisting young married women. Usually I take it upon myself to approach the police if their help is required. When necessary, we can get the help of a lawyer as there is an advocate who volunteers to come to our office once a week and give legal advice. In recent years we have been especially concerned about the burning of young wives for dowry. Sometimes we organize demonstrations against the authorities because justice is not being done. We have also helped a very large number of deserted wives get maintenance allowance for themselves and their children. This work is still continuing.

The Indian Council for Child Welfare is our most important organization for looking after children. The headquarters of this council is in New Delhi and acts as a guiding and directing agency. It is in the state that the actual work is carried out. The Central Council does undertake certain projects such as the all-India camp for children. It also focuses the attention of the authorities and the public on the need to help disabled children and provide programs for school dropouts.

In 1957, at Indira Gandhi's suggestion, the Indian Council for Child Welfare developed a way of recognizing the brave deeds of children. Every year children who have committed heroic deeds are brought to Delhi where the Prime Minister awards medals and certificates. The Ministry of Railways participates by issuing free railway passes and the Ministry of Defense further honors them by making them an integral part of the Republic Day Parade on January 26.

The Ministry of Social Welfare awards each of the children a cash grant and the Ministry of Education reserves three seats in Medical College, and five in the Engineering College—three for the degree and two for the diploma in engineering. Because most of these children are from rural areas, this recognition is seen as an honor to their village as well.

Another important area of work for the council is in adoption. Many Indian babies are adopted by foreigners. I went to visit some to see for myself how these children were coping when I visited Switzerland, Norway, and Sweden as the President of the Indian Council for Child Welfare. It did my heart good to see how well the children had settled into their new homes and the love and affection showered on them by their adoptive parents. Lately, Indian families have also started adopting such children, but this had not been our custom previously.

I have been actively connected with the *Arya Anathalaya* (an orphanage) since 1950. It was established by Swami Shraddhanand back in 1918 after an epidemic of influenza that left some boys and girls bereft of one or both parents. Since the breaking up of the joint family system, such institutions have become necessary in our country. There are no longer large homes where one or two distant relations can be housed. The *Arya Anathalaya* has grown rapidly. It houses over six hundred boys and girls. We feed, clothe, and educate them, and when they reach adulthood we see that they are settled in life.

I was the President of the Family Planning Association of Delhi for nine years. Part of our work was to go out to the rural areas to try to convince people to limit the size of their families. It was an uphill task, and still is. The population is growing by leaps and bounds, partly because of poverty. Families feel they need more pairs of hands to contribute to their total income. Besides, there are very few health centers in rural areas. Now more attention is being given to the newborn child, but twenty years ago it was difficult for people in villages to get any assistance if their child fell ill. Expecting that some would die, the parents wanted more children. They believed that out of twelve children perhaps three would survive until adulthood. As Hindus they believed that they had to have a son who could look after them in old age and, what is more important, perform their last rites on their demise. These attitudes are the most difficult to change. Even though families are breaking up and scattering all over the world, tradition is hard to break. Only widespread education will ultimately result in changed attitudes toward the number and sex of children desired.

I remember that during the war with China, we were almost thrown out of a village when we advocated birth control. People told us that the country needed manpower for its armed forces. How could we expect them to limit their families? It amused us that the villagers argued against family planning by suggesting that China would wait quietly for twenty years until newborn boys could grow up and join the armed forces.

In 1967–68 we were asked by the government to disband the Family Planning Association in spite of the good work we were doing. The government thought they were better equipped to handle population control and wanted one policy. I have always felt that social problems can be handled better by voluntary workers who are more dedicated and can approach issues on a more personal level. I also feel that our growing population is such a major problem that it threatens the country's future, and that, in fact, it should be tackled on a warlike footing.

The Delhi Commonwealth Women's Association came into existence in 1952. I have been working with them for more than forty years. The aim was and still is to have contact with the women of Commonwealth countries residing in Delhi and jointly plan welfare activities for the poor and the needy. Since the association's inception, the members have been both Indians and foreigners and have worked together very harmoniously. We have donated medicine and clothing to poor patients in various hospitals in Delhi and provided wheelchairs and other necessities to people with disabilities. The association has constructed it own building in the nearby village of Zamrudpur. At this medical center, patients are treated for free by a team of dedicated and qualified doctors who volunteer their services. In addition, the association runs small schools for village children and classes in sewing and tailoring for women.

This is a very brief account of a few of the welfare organizations in which I have been actively involved for many years. There are many others that I have not mentioned here, but it does not mean that they are not important or that I have little or no interest in them. My activities will continue for the rest of my life.

Epilogue

With the completion of my memoirs, an important phase of my life is over. Lately my life has had many ups and downs. It is almost twenty years since I lost my husband, and I miss his companionship and advice.

Late in 1977, my only son went to Nairobi, Kenya, to serve as the Chair of a firm called Ideal Casements Ltd. I received weekly letters from him full of exciting and interesting news, telling me how much he was enjoying his work. He was holding weekly meetings with the heads of various sections of the company and making new friends. But tragedy struck the family again, and in less than three months he passed away in the prime of his life. His wife and children, a girl and a boy, moved to her parents' home, leaving me alone in the apartment in New Delhi.

Fortunately my two daughters are happily married and settled in their respective homes in Delhi. The eldest, Anjali, is a practicing lawyer and has the distinction of being a partner in an all-male law firm. She was the first woman lawyer in northern India to achieve this status.

My younger daughter, Saloni, is a versatile writer in English. She has produced a book of short stories and a novel based on the Indian struggle for freedom.

I continue to live alone and am still actively associated with various social welfare organizations; most of them date back to 1950–52, so I have been able to observe how far we have come and what still needs to be done. It distresses me to no end to find that even after forty years of independence we are not yet able to provide all the people of this country with the basic services—shelter, electricity, water, and education. It seems that our leaders are still groping in the dark trying to decide what kind of country they want India to be—democratic? socialist? capitalist? or some combination? In the meantime, who suffers? Always the common people.

Unfortunately Gandhiji's teachings are completely forgotten. On his birthday, October 2, the nation pays lip service to him, and that seems to be all that is done. I believe that my countrymen, though illiterate, have enough determination that given the right direction they can pull the country out of this mire. At present the leaders all seem consumed with their own concerns. There are times when I feel very strongly that my going in and out of prison during my youth was a sacrifice in vain.

Yet I also feel that in the very near future my country will shake off its present lethargy and India will join the progressive nations of the world. The tragedy for me is that I may not be here to witness it.

Manmohini Sahgal
New Delhi, August 1993

Glossary

anna one-sixteenth of a rupee

ashram colony, a place where a community of people who share an ideology live together

bhai brother

bhabi sister-in-law

chappal sandal

charka spinning wheel

dal cooked lentils

Diwali festival of lights, celebrated in October or November

Eid Muslim celebration that marks the end of Ramadan, the month when the Prophet Muhammad first received the word of Allah

harijan "Child of God," Gandhi's name for those people who belonged to castes the British labeled "untouchable"

hartal cessation of work because the soul is suffering; a strike for moral reasons

Holi a spring festival that includes singing, dancing, feasting, and the throwing of colored powder and water on friends and relatives

jawan soldier

ji an honorific suffix added to names

khadi hand-spun, hand-woven cloth

lakh one hundred thousand

lathi a metal-tipped stick used by the police

lota water pitcher used by an individual for his/her ablutions

mantras sacred verses

Mughal Emperor the Mughals, Muslims from Central Asia, ruled in northern India from the fifteenth to the eighteenth century

munshi court clerk

nagar small town

pandal marquee

pandit priest, or man who belongs to a priestly caste

pice or *paisa* one-sixty-fourth of a rupee

puja act of worship generally involving an image or symbol of the god or goddess

roti flat, unleavened bread

rupee Indian currency

satyagraha term used by Gandhi to describe his ideology and tactics for nonviolent but aggressive protest; truth force

Srimati a respectful form of address used for women, used as the equivalent of "Mrs."

swadeshi made in the country

swaraj self-rule

takli a knitting-needle-like apparatus for spinning

tonga a horse-drawn cart that carries four to five people; used in northern India

tongawalla *tonga* driver

Index

Achabal (India), 36
Adoption, 153
Ahmed, Bashir, 49
Ahmed, Lady Sultan, 113
Alam, Mohammad, 90
Alfred Theatrical Company, 25
Ali, Aruna Asaf, 114, 138
Ali, Manzar, 6
Allahabad (India), xiii, 6
Allahabad University, 98
All-India Congress, 58–59, 107, 109
All India Village and Khadi Industries Organization, 29
All-India Women's Central Food Council, 150–51
All-India Women's Conference (AIWC), 113
Ambalvi, Lala Duni Chand, 135, 143
American Women's Club, 130
Amritsar (India), 13–14
Ananda Math (Chatterjee), 30
Anand Bhavan (Allahabad), xiii, 3, 4, 29, 116
Andrews, C.F., 14
Annapurna Cafeteria, 150–51
Arrest methods, 91
Arya Anathalaya, 153–54
Asian Relations Conference, 122
Atal, Arjan Nath, 24
Azad, Chandra Shekhar, 63–64, 90
Azad, Maulana Abul-Kalam, 58–59, 138, 140–41

Bagga, Indar Lal, 147
Bagh Kare Khan (Delhi), 146–47
Bai, Maharani Setu Parvati, 121
Baker, Herbert, 106

Bali, Dina Nath, 21
Bali, Sushila, 21
Banerjea, B.N., 126
Banerjea, Kamola, 34
Banerjea, Shanta, 8
Barker, Colonel, 94
Barrackpore (Calcutta), 109
Basant panchami day, 8
Belgian Sisters of Charity, 10
Bengal, xiv
Bewoor, Lady, 125
Bhabha, C.H., 123
Bhandari, Padma, 108
Bharat Mein Augrezi Raj (Lal), 63
Bhartiya Mahila Craft Society, 131
Bihar (India), 99–103
Bihar Female School. *See* Bihar *Mahila Vidyapith*
Bihar *Mahila Vidyapith*, xix-xx, 99–103
Birla, Raja Baldeo Dass, 109
Birla temple, 109–10
Bombay (India), xiv, 115, 117–23
Bose, Subhash Chandra, 65, 109
Boycotts, xiii, 28
Burma, 104

Calcutta (India), 105, 108–09
Caste associations, xiv
Censorship, 14
Central Electric Power Authority, 123
Champaran District (Bihar), 12
Chand, Bakshi Tek, 54–55, 135
Chand, Gopi, 46–47, 48
Chandra, Kailash, 132, 133
Chandra, Pravin, 118
Chappals, 18, 102

162 INDEX

Charan, Durga Bhagwati, 41, 51, 64, 93, 94–95
Charka, 17
Chatterjee, Bankim Chandra, 30
Chattopadhyay, Shrimati Kamaledevi, 17
Chaudhri, Rambhaj Dutt, 16
Chaudhurani, Shrimati Saraladevi, 15–16
Chauri Chaura (Uttar Pradesh), 17–18
Chawla, Shakuntal, 73
Child marriages, 101–02
Children, 130–31, 153–54
Chopra, P.D., 78, 94
Clothing, 20
  See also *Khadi*; *Swadeshi*
College of Catering, 151
Committee to Change Food Habits, 151
Communal Award (1932), 89, 89*n*.
Connaught Place (New Delhi), 106
Cripps, Stafford, 121
Cub Scouts, 119–20
Custodian of Evacuee Property, 133

Dalhousie (India), 37
Dara, J.S., 148, 149
Das, C.R., 28
Das, Jatin, 51, 64, 65
Das, Kiren Chandra, 51, 65
Das, Lala Pinda, 95
Deen Dayal Upadhyaya Marg (Delhi), 147
Defense of India Act, 13
Delhi (India), 124, 136
Delhi Commonwealth Women's Association, 154–55
Delhi Gate (police station), 61
De Montmorency, Geoffrey, 86–87
Deshmukh, Durgabai, 141
Devi, Shrimati Pooran, 62, 73
Dhebar, U.N., 140–41, 142
Disney, C.H., 73, 74–75
Diwali (festival), 102
Domestic science, 32
Dulari, Raj, 134
Dunnicliffe, H.B., 54–55
Dutt, B.K., 64, 65

Dutt, Mrs. B.C., 121
Dyer, R.E., 13–14

Education, 7, 9–10, 30–39
  for women, xiv, xvii, xix
  See also Vocational training
Elections, 135–44

Famine, 12
Farmers, 12–13
Food grains, 150
Forman Christian College, 41, 67–70

Ganderbal (India), 36
Gandhi, Indira, 144, 153
Gandhi, Mohandas K., 14, 25–26, 91
  arrest, 12
  and boycotts, 28
  harijan work, 96–97
  at Lahore Congress, 50
  march against Salt Law, 51, 56–57
  noncooperation movement, 17–18
  and nonviolence, 93
  and picketing, 58
  return from South Africa, xv
  role in mobilizing women, xix
  and Rowlatt Bills, 13
  satyagraha movement, xvi, 88, 89
  village industries program, 22, 29
Gandhi–Irwin Pact, 88, 89–90
Gandhi, Rajiv, 144
Gandhi Nagar Mahila Colony, 131
Ganges River, 102
Garhwal Battalion, 62
Garrett, H.L.O., 54, 56, 69, 86
Gauba, Jawan Lal, 110
Gautam, R., 126
George VI (king of England), 105
Ghora Khal (hill station), 26–27
Girls' club. See *Kumari sabha*
Government College for Men (Lahore), 40–41, 55–56, 67–70
Gujrat (India), 79–80
Gupta, Desh Bandhu, 136
Guru, Raj, 63–64, 67, 90–91
Gurunath, Sir, 125

Handoo, Chandra Zutshi, 9, 15, 18, 21, 26, 84, 113
  bachelor's degree, 28
  leaving of school, 31
  marriage, 22–23
Handoo, Krishna, 22–23, 113
Harijans, 89, 96–97, 148–49
Harijan Welfare Board, 29
Hartal, 13, 67–68
Hathi, Jai Sukhlal, 152
Hill Grange School (Bombay), 118, 119
Hindi Prachar Sabha, 118
Hindu Marriage Reform League, xv
Hindustani Seva Dal, 44
Hindustan Republican Army, 63–64
Hindustan Socialist Republican Association, 64
Horniman, B.G., 14
Hotels, 151
Hunger strike, 65

Imperial Bank, 132
Income Tax Appellate Tribunal, 114–15
Independence Day, 51–52
India Act (1909). *See* Morley–Minto reforms
Indian Council for Child Welfare, 153
Indian National Congress, 15
  Calcutta session, 42, 43
  and Gandhi, xvi
  Lahore session, 43–52
  and Muslim League, 121, 123
  women's issues, xxi
International Council of Women, 105
Irwin, Lord, 59–60, 88
Iyer, Mr., 44

Jain, Ajit Prasad, 128–29, 133, 136
Jallianwala Bagh (Amritsar), 13–14
Jayakar, M.R., 60
Jesus and Mary Convent (Delhi), 110
Jesus and Mary Convent (Lahore), 9
Joshi, Subhadra, 141–42

Kailasanand, Swami, 110
Kapur, Jawan Lal, 67–68, 71

Kapur, Trilok Chand, 44
Kashmir, 8, 125
Kasturba Niketan (Delhi), 130–31
Kaul, Bal Kishan, 21
Kaur, Amar, 91, 152
Kaur, Rajkumari Amrit, 113, 142, 146
Kaur, Rup, 79
Khadi, 17, 18–20, 22
Khan, Abdul Majid, 42, 43
Khan, Hakim Ajmal, 26, 28
Khan, Khan Abdul Gaffar, 89
Khan, Liaquat Ali, 123
Khan, Zulfiqur Ali, 16
Khanna, M.L., 133
Khanna, Mehr Chand, 136, 137, 152
Khanna, Santosh, xviii
Khas tatties, 112
Kidwai, Rafi Ahmed, 135, 136
Kinnaird College, 23, 31, 32–35
Kisan Mazdoor Praja, 136
Kishan, Hari, 87
Kishan, Ram, 51
Kishore, Dewan Kishan, 11–12
Kishore, Naval, 133
Kotwal, 3
Kripalani, Acharya J.B., 136, 142
Kripalani, Sucheta K., 126, 136–42, 149
Kumari, Swadesh, 68, 70–71
Kumari sabha, 8, 12

"Ladies' parties," 113
Lady Maclagan School for Girls, 31
Lahore (India), xv, 9, 41
Lahore College for Women, 31–32, 68
Lahore Conspiracy Case (1927), 41, 64–65, 67, 90
Lahore Female Jail, 61, 76
Lahore Student Union, 41–43, 53–54
Lal, Harkishan Lala, 44
Lal, Hira, 20–21
Lal, Sunder, 63
Langhorne, Professor, 55
Law College (Lahore), 68–70
Lawrence, Pethwick, 121
Lewis, Edgar, 61, 71
Luytens, Edward, 106

Maclagan Engineering College
  (Mughulpura), 53–54
Madras (India), xiv
Mahajan, Mehr Chand, 139
Mahila sammelan, 8, 11–12
Maintenance Allowance Scheme, 128
Mal, Rai Bahadur Boota, 6
Malaviya, Krishna Kant, 98
Mango leaves, 118
Mantras, 8
Marriage, 101–02
Martial law, 14
Mathai, John, 128
Mathai, M.O., 141
Menon, Krishna, 130, 143
Militants, xiii
Ministry of Rehabilitation, 123, 124–34
Misra, Ram Nandan, 99, 100, 102, 103
Mitter, B.L., 113
Modern School (Delhi), 110
Mohan, Sushila, 93–94
Montagu, Edwin, xv
Montagu–Chelmsford Reforms, xv
Morley–Minto reforms, xiii
Mountbatten, Lady, 126
Movies, 9
Mukerjee, B.K., 139
Munshi, K.M., 150
Munshi, Lilavati, 150, 151
Music, 9, 39
Muslim League, 121, 123
Muslim Women's Transit Camp, 126–27

Naidu, Sarojini, 16, 59
Nanda, D.C., 132, 133, 148
Narang, Chanda, xxiii
Nath, Bola, 94
Nath, Raja Narendra, 37
Nath, Rani Narendra, 16, 23
Nath, Sham, 145, 146
National Council of Women in India (NCWI), 105–06, 113, 121
National Federation of Indian Women, 152–53
NCWI. *See* National Council of Women in India

Nehru, Biharilal, 3
Nehru, Braj Lal, 23
Nehru, Gangadhar, 3–4
Nehru, Indrani, 4
Nehru, Jawaharlal, 4, 6, 16, 109, 131, 148–49
  arrest, 89
  Asian Relations Conference, 122
  on Bhagat Singh, 91
  education, xiv
  and Gandhi–Irwin Pact, 90
  at Lahore session, 43–48
  as Prime Minister, 123
  in prison, 72
  and Sahgal's candidacy, xxi, 135, 137, 140, 141, 143
  and Salt Law protest, 57
  wedding, 7–8
Nehru, Kamla, 28, 37, 72
Nehru, Krishna, xiv
Nehru, Maharani, 4
Nehru, Mohan Lal, 3, 115–16
Nehru, Motilal, xiii–xiv, xviii, 3–6, 8, 26–27, 29
  Indian National Congress, 15, 42
  and Lahore Conspiracy Case, 65
  in prison, 72
  Swaraj party, 28
Nehru, Nandalal, 3, 4
Nehru, Patrani, xiv, 4
Nehru, Rameshwari, xiv–xv, 124, 126–27, 127
Nehru, Shyam Lal, 15
Nehru, Uma, 15, 72
Neogy, K.C., 124, 126
New Delhi (India), 104–16, 120
New Delhi Municipal Committee, 149
Northern Railway Employees' Union, 145
Norton, Eardley, 14

O'Brian, Colonel, 14
O'Dwyer, Michael, 15
Ordinance rule, 89, 89*n*., 91

Pakistan, 125
Pan, 7
Pandit, A.D., 149

INDEX   165

Pandit, Ranjit S., 22, 24, 62
Pandit, Vijayalakshmi, xiv, 22, 24, 72
Pant, Govind Vallabh, 136
Partition, xx
Patel, Vithal Bhai, 62
Pathak, Gopal Swaroop, 138
Peasants and Workers party. *See*
   Kisan Mazdoor Praja
Peshawar Inquiry Committee Report,
   62–63
Picketing, 58, 68
Police, 14
Prakash, Chaudhury Brahm, 136, 137
Prasad, Ganga, 132
Prasad, Jagdish, 113
Prasad, Rajendra, 101, 130
Premchand, Tarabai, 121
Presentation Convent (Delhi), 110
Prison, 72–85
   inspections in, 78
   for women, xviii–xix
Prisoners
   political, 88
   pretrial, 65–66
Prithivi Raj Market (New Delhi), 149
Punjab, 9, 57
Punjab University, 42, 86
Punjab University Act, 55
Puri, N.D., 83
Pushpa puja, 8

Queen Mary's College (Lahore), 9

Radhakrishan, S., 86–87
Rai, Lala Lajpat, 46, 63, 70, 72
Railroads, 23, 145–46
Raina, Chand Narayan, 26
Raina, Madan Mohan, 24
Raina, Raja Atal, 26
Raina, Shiv Narayan, 25
Raj, Mrs. Hem, 32
Raj, Raizada Hans, 89
Raj, Sukhdev, 41, 67, 90–91
Ram, Beli, 20
Ram, Bindi, 147
Ram, Ladha, 79
Ram, Udho, 21
Rangoon (Burma), 104

Rani, Raj, 70
Rao, Benegal Rama, 22
Rashid, Abdul, 11
Rashid, Marzia, 11
Ravi River, 57
Ray, Renuka, xx, 141
Razdan, Mrs. Bishan Narain, 5
"Red Leaflet," 64
Refugees, 126–28, 147
Religion, xiii
Repression, 93
Restaurants, 151
Round Table Conference (London), 89
Rowlatt Bills (1919), xv, 13
Rowlatt, F.A., 13
Roy, B.C., xx
R.S. Bhola Ram and Sons, 58
Russell, Dudley, 125
Russell, Elizabeth, 125

Sacred Heart Convent (Lahore), 10,
   12, 30–31, 32
Sadhana, 17
Sahgal, Amrit Lal, xx, 98–99, 114–15,
   124
Sahgal, Anjali, 110–11, 1567
Sahgal, Manmohini Zutshi
   arrests, 67–85, 88
   background, xiii–xxiv
   in Bombay, 117–23
   candidacies, 135–44
   doctoral studies, 122
   early life, 3–10
   education, 21–22, 30–39, 40–41, 122
   fighting the raj, 86–97
   at Lahore Congress, 43–52
   leadership skills, xvii, xviii–xix
   marriage, xx, 103
   at Ministry of Rehabilitation, 123,
      124–34
   mother and family, 11–29
   in New Delhi and Simla, 104–16
   new life, 98–103
   and political office, xxi
   in prison, 72–85, 88, 93
   refugee work, xx, 124–34
   and *satyagraha* movement, 53–66
   swimming lessons, 120–21

166 INDEX

Sahgal, Manmohini Zutshi *(continued)*
  teaching position, xix–xx, 99–103
  trial, 74–76
  trip to Gujrat, 79–81
  typhoid fever, 20–21
  vacation activities, 35–39
  welfare work, 145–55
Sahgal, Pradip, 108–11, 119–20, 125, 156
Sahgal, Saloni, 118–19, 125, 156
St. Columbus School (Delhi), 110
St. Mary's Convent (Allahabad), 7
St. Xavier's College (Bombay), 122–23
Salt Law, 51, 56–57, 62
Santanam, Pandit K., 48, 54, 90
Sapru, Tej Bahadur, 60
Saran, Raksha, 124, 126
Sati, xvi
Satyagraha movement, xvi, 51, 53–66, 72
  end of, xix, 88, 89, 98
Saunders, J.P., 64
Saxena, Mohanlal, 128
Scott, J.A., 63–64
Second All-Punjab Student Conference, 42–43
Sen, Hannah, 124, 126, 127
Senior citizens, 127–28
Servants of the People Society, 46
Seth, Govind H., 132–33
Sethi, Suchinta, 126
Setna, Bachi, 41
Shafi, Mohammad, 17
Shastri, Lal Bahadur, 137, 138–39, 140, 147
Shraddhanand, Swami, 95*n*, 153
Simla (India), 59–60, 104–16
Simla Congress Committee, 59
Simon, John, 63
Singhara atta, 150
Singh, Bai Mohan, 149
Singh, Chanan, 87
Singh, Sardar Karnail, 145
Singh, Sardar Kishan, 90
Singh, Sardar Mangal, 44, 45, 48
Singh, Sardool, 79

Singh, Shaheed Bhagat, 41, 63–65, 67, 90–91
Sirajuddin, Joyce, 41
Snowball Club, 125
Socialism, 64
Social Welfare Rehabilitation Directorate, 128
Sondhi, Colonel, 89
Sri Darpan (journal), xiv-xv
Sri Ramkrishna Mission, 110
Strike. *See Hartal*
Sudan, Prem Lata, 41
Suggarmal, Bakshi, 73
Swadeshi, xiii, 3, 17
Swaraj Bhavan. See Anand Bhavan (Allahabad)
Swaraj party, 27–28
Swastheya Committee, 146

Tagore, Rabindra Nath, 30
Tandon, Sampuran Singh, 79, 94
Tata School for Social Sciences (Bombay), 35
Taxes, 12
Textile industry, 19
Thapar, Prem, 122
Tikku, Jeevan Lal, 5
Tilak, Lokmanya, 52
"Train outrage," 51

Unions, 145–46
United Council for Relief and Welfare, 126
United Nations, 143
Upadhyaya, S.K., 48, 129
Usury, 148

"*Vande Mataram*" (anthem), 30–31, 50
Varma, N.L., 59
Vati, Kumari Lajja, 44, 45, 48, 50
Vati, Satya, 74
Village industries. *See* All India Village and Khadi Industries Organization
Virindra, Dhanwantry, 51
Vocational training, 131–32

Weddings, 8, 22–23, 24
Willingdon, Lord, 89, 104–05
Women, 5–6, 24–25, 49, 93, 152–53
  betrayal of, xxi–xxii
  discrimination against, xvi
  education, xiv, xvii, xix
  independence movement, xix
  inequities, xvi–xvii
  prison life for, xviii–xix, 76–77
  restricted life of, 18
  seclusion, xiv
  and unions, 146
  vocational training for, 131–32
Women's club. *See Mahila sammelan*
Woolner, A.C., 87
World War II, 114

Yashpal, 51

Zafar, Bahadur Shah, 3
Zaidi, Begum Qudsia, 149
Zutshi, Chandra. *See* Handoo, Chandra Zutshi
Zutshi, Janak, 10, 18, 23, 28, 38, 42
  arrest, 92

Zutshi, Janak *(continued)*
  release from prison, 95
  resignation, 70–71
  at school, 31
  teaching position, xviii, 40, 68
Zutshi, Ladli Prasad, xiv, 3, 4, 5, 6–7, 56, 75–76, 115–16
Zutshi, Lado Rani, xiv, xv, xvi, 5, 8–9, 11–29, 42, 143
  as all-India Dictator, 58–59
  arrest of, 61–62, 73
  in prison, 74, 76–78, 84–85, 89, 93, 95
  release, 96
  and Sacred Heart Convent, 30–31
Zutshi, Lalji Prasad, xiv, 4–5
Zutshi, Manmohini. *See* Sahgal, Manmohini Zutshi
Zutshi, Shyama, 9, 19, 28, 38, 50, 57, 96
  arrest, 68, 70–71, 72, 92
  at college, 23, 40, 41
  birth of, 6
  release from prison, 95
  withdrawal from school, 30–31, 32

Manmohini Zutshi Sahgal was born in 1909 in Allahabad, India, in *Anand Bhavan*, the home of the great nationalist leader Pandit Motilal Nehru. While Manmohini was studying for her M.A. at Government College (a men's college) in Lahore, she became the first female president of the Lahore Students Union. Defying government orders, Manmohini led demonstrations that resulted in her arrest in 1930. She was jailed three times (in 1930, 1931, and 1932) for her political activity. In 1935 Manmohini accepted a position running a girls' school in Bihar, but left it to marry Mr. Amrit Lal Sahgal, a chartered accountant and officer in the Government of India. During these years Manmohini bore three children, dabbled in politics, became a union leader, and worked as a volunteer with social welfare organizations.

Geraldine Forbes is professor of history at the State University of New York, Oswego. She is author of *Positivism in Bengal*, editor of *The Memoirs of an Indian Woman* by Shudha Mazumdar, and the series editor of "Foremother Legacies: Autobiographies and Memoirs of Women from Asia, Africa, the Middle East, and Latin America." She has written numerous articles on the history of Indian women in the later half of the nineteenth century and early decades of the twentieth century. She teaches courses in Asian history and women's studies.